ANGLICAN CHURCH-BUILDING IN LONDON 1915–1945

ANGLICAN CHURCH-BUILDING IN LONDON 1915-1945

Michael Yelton
and
John Salmon

Spire Books Ltd

PO Box 2336. Reading RG4 5WJ
www.spirebooks.com

Spire Books Ltd
PO Box 2336
Reading RG4 5WJ
www.spirebooks.com

Copyright © 2007
Spire Books Ltd,
Michael Yelton and
John Salmon

CIP data:
A catalogue record for this book is available
from the British Library
ISBN 978-1-904965-14-5

Designed and produced by John Elliott
Text set in Adobe Bembo

Printed by Hobbs the Printers Ltd
Totton, Hampshire

Illustration opposite title page: St Saviour, Acton, by Maufe (1924).

Production of this book has been assisted by a financial contribution from the Anglo-Catholic History Society.

CONTENTS

St Barnabas, North Ealing, Font and East End, E.C. Shearman (1916)

INTRODUCTION

Inter-war churches are at the present time neither popular nor much discussed. They appear to occupy a similar position to that held by Victorian churches only sixty years ago, even in the minds of those interested in architecture. It is perhaps appreciated that a very large number were built, especially during the ten years prior to the outbreak of the Second World War, but they are little praised. Schemes to modify them, and in particular to remove the distinctive period feel which some still exhibit, attract little interest. They are inadequately catalogued, and often hidden in suburban back streets.

There are of course some exceptions to these general statements. The Twentieth Century Society (formerly the Thirties Society) has done sterling work in raising awareness of buildings of the period. In London in particular, the more recent *Buildings of England* volumes, especially that on East London, have devoted much more attention to churches erected during the period in question: earlier editions and particularly the originals as prepared by Pevsner himself, rarely have more than a line or two on any inter-war ecclesiastical buildings, and many of them are simply ignored. There are many general books on London churches, nearly all of which have in recent years gone beyond concentration on mediaeval survivals and included a selection of the better nineteenth-century and Edwardian buildings. However, the post-1914 period is usually given only a token mention, with reference to, and perhaps pictures of, two or three of the better known inter-war churches, such as St Saviour, Eltham or St Thomas, Hanwell. There is one notable exception to that general neglect, which is Kenneth Richardson's pioneering and detailed study of the Twenty-Five Churches Campaign in the Diocese of Southwark, as devised and executed by the administratively able Bishop C.F. Garbett. Richardson's book, published by the Ecclesiological Society in 2002, set new standards for work in this field.

Very little has, by contrast with the Victorians, been written about any of the leading ecclesiastical architects of the age: on, for example, N.F. Cachemaille-Day, consistently the most original such designer, almost nothing is available.

The future of a number of the churches listed in the gazetteer is doubtful. Whereas some have large and lively congregations and organisations which reach out to their local populations, others appear neglected and little used. One or two indeed see more use by so-called 'Community Churches' than by the Church of England itself, which retains only a marginal presence in its own building. These churches are at serious risk and they have few friends to defend them. It may be that this book will assist in raising awareness of their plight and in increasing interest in all the period has to offer.

One of the problems with appreciation of churches built between the wars is their location. The enormous growth in the built-up area of cities, particularly London (although in fact most of the new houses were constructed outside the LCC boundary) was around the periphery. In London, no new Anglican churches were built in the 1915-45 period in the Cities of London or Westminster. On the other hand in Ealing or Harrow, or even more so in Becontree, large numbers of new churches were built to cater for the extraordinarily rapid increase in population in the

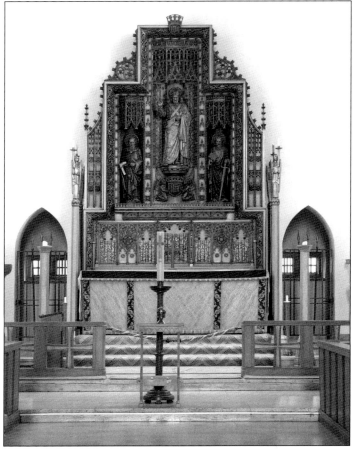

St Thomas, Hanwell (1934): high altar by Hare, from St Thomas, Portman Square.

The two best contemporary source-books are the volumes published by the Incorporated Church Building Society, *New Churches Illustrated* in 1936, depicting buildings erected from about the mid 1920s onwards, and *Fifty Modern Churches* in 1947, dealing with the 1930-45 period, both of which are readily available in the second-hand market. They each show buildings scarcely finished and in particular with little landscaping or foliage around. The visitor today will find many of the same churches little externally altered, but very difficult to see at long distance because they are now almost completely surrounded by mature tree growth. Leafy, now a clichéd adjective for 1930s suburbs, is in fact an accurate description of many such areas.

The scope of this study

A word or two of justification is perhaps required in relation to those parameters. The Greater London area is convenient, not only because it is clearly defined and widely understood, but also because it does in general terms correspond with the built-up metropolitan area. The decision to confine the book to Anglican churches was taken partly on pragmatic grounds, in that otherwise the research required would have been so great as to mean that the book would take many years to compile, and partly because the variety of churches built even by the Church of England alone is such to provide plenty of interest. Perhaps others will follow with catalogues of Roman Catholic and Nonconformist buildings in the area.

The timescale was taken from 1915, on the basis that many studies end in 1914 and there were a few churches which were in the course of being constructed or planned when the First World War broke out. Unlike the Second World War, there was little destruction of property from enemy action in the years 1914-8, although one church (St Augustine of Hippo,

outer ring of the capital. People do not, on the whole, visit 1930s suburbs to sightsee and, if they do, they will find it impossible to visit the interior of any but a few churches without an appointment in advance. Nonetheless the churches described in this book have however now acquired some of the status which comes from age and permanence, and we can look at them in that light of the perspective. The aim of this volume is to provide a gazetteer of and introduction to new Anglican church building from 1915 to 1945 in what is now the Greater London area.

Leytonstone) was burnt out after being the recipient of a fire bomb from a Zeppelin and St Barnabas, West Silvertown, was replaced by a completely new building after the original was destroyed in the munitions explosion of 1917 which devastated the surrounding area. At the other end of the period, there are a number of churches which, rather surprisingly, were completed or even constructed after the commencement of hostilities in 1939, including St Patrick, Barking, which was in an area where bombing was very heavy. By 1942 however church building had ceased and did not begin again until the 1950s, another era where the number of new churches is commonly understated.

In the immediate post-First World War period, money was in short supply and few new churches were constructed. In the 1920s, a number of new ones were erected in areas where the population was beginning to expand, such as St Mary, Sanderstead, and St John the Divine, Romford, and the Southwark drive set out below began to take effect from the middle of the decade.

It was however to be the 1930s which was to prove

St Thomas, Hanwell (1934) by Maufe, Lady chapel.

one of the most prolific decades for church building in the modern era. Nearly the whole of Middlesex was covered with suburban development, as well as parts of Hertfordshire, Essex, Kent and Surrey. The church authorities were well aware of the problems posed by these new communities and were anxious to build as soon as possible. Very often temporary premises came first, sometimes using marquees or the like, to be followed by dual-purpose church/halls. In due course permanent churches were erected alongside many of the halls, and the latter ceased to be used for services. Others remain to this day as the place of worship, undemonstrative buildings which do not proclaim themselves to passers-by but at least are cheap to heat and run and can be used for secular purposes during the week. St Cedd, Barkingside, is one such, as is St James the Great, Blendon, but perhaps this genre is best illustrated by the unprepossessing St Agnes, Romford, where the Sunday mass succeeds the Saturday dancing class. Even where permanent new churches were built, the plans are often far more imposing than the building which was actually erected: the number of cases where towers were planned but never added is legion. The fact that successive churches were erected on the same site raises problems of definition, in that the 'new' churches described in this book are obviously primarily the permanent buildings built as long-term provision for the areas in question. They also include those buildings, such as St Cedd, Barkingside, mentioned above, where although there was a plan for a more imposing edifice, and in that case a prospective site was available, no such church was ever erected. In many places the first hall/church was replaced, either by a new building erected between the wars or in the 1950s. These are dealt with in the book, although for obvious reasons they receive rather less detailed attention than those in other categories, and there may well be others, often short-lived, which have been missed. Lastly, there are

a number of instances where substantial rebuilding took place, usually by the provision of a new chancel or nave, which have again been included. In any such list, there are inevitably marginal cases and if some have been omitted which others consider should be included, an apology is tendered. St Jude, Hampstead Garden Suburb, is sometimes listed as a post-First World War church, but is not in this book, on the basis that it was largely completed before 1915 although work remained to be done thereafter. Its spirit was definitely of the Edwardian era. The dates quoted are also sometimes less exact than appears, since sometimes churches opened before they were fully completed, and were then consecrated later still, so various dates are quoted in different sources.

Funding new churches

The chief problem facing the Church in its response to the urgent need for new buildings was of course a lack of money. The editor of *New Churches Illustrated* specifically commented in his preface that 'It is much to be regretted that architects should sometimes be asked or expected to design churches for a sum far below an essential minimum'. In a number of cases, the desire for haste led to unsatisfactory building practices and later problems, especially with damp.

There were campaigns for finance in all the relevant dioceses: the most ambitious was the Diocese of London's Forty-Five Churches Fund, sponsored by the much-loved but administratively incompetent Bishop A.F. Winnington-Ingram, who during his long episcopate (1901–39) saw 79 new churches consecrated and 38 enlarged, many of course before the period with which this book is concerned. The progress of the Forty-Five Churches Fund is rather more difficult to chronicle, in that, as the Bishop's biographer tactfully put it: '[Winnington-Ingram's] optimism sometimes led him to use figures in what grammarians call a proleptic sense, in which the future is mingled with the present, and it is hard to distinguish what is hoped for from what has been achieved.' By 1938, however, the Secretary of the Fund reported that there were 63 new districts identified, and in 53 of these there were halls. In addition, in 16 permanent churches had been consecrated, with another 8 about to be started.[1]

As already mentioned, the Diocese of Southwark, under the able but sometimes autocratic leadership of Garbett, had a more modest but attainable target of 25 new churches, which was well planned and generally

St Barnabas, Temple Fortune (1932) by E. C Shearman.

competently executed from 1925 until the mid-1930s, rather earlier than that in London, which reflected the way the South London estates were developed: Garbett actually left the Diocese in 1932 for Winchester with most of the work done. In the Diocese of Chelmsford, which was carved out of St Albans only in 1914, the new Bishop took over the direction of the London Over the Border Fund, which was placed under huge strain by the rapid growth in population of the Dagenham and Becontree estates. There was a similar but more modest Twelve Churches Scheme in the Diocese of Rochester, covering the new suburbs of Kent, and other areas where expansion took place came under the jurisdictions of the Bishop of St Albans (Barnet) and of the Archbishop of Canterbury (Croydon). It is unfortunate that there appears to have been little cooperation between the relevant Dioceses to plan coherently, and assistance from rural Dioceses which did not need to build was very rare: there was one notable exception, in that the Diocese of Hereford raised a high proportion of the costs involved in the new church of SS. George & Ethelbert, East Ham.

It is ironic in the light of the great efforts which were made to provide the new churches that in many cases they were filled, if at all, for a relatively short time. The Church of England had a period which we can now see as a false dawn during the 1950s in which congregations and vocations increased modestly but steadily. This emboldened some to finish the work which had been started in the 1930s, by adding large and expensive extensions to complete churches of that era. It is now clear that the Church overreached itself, and very soon regretted the increase in building which had taken place, as well as finding the burden of paying pensions for the bulge in the number of clergy difficult to sustain. One very clear example of this development is St Barnabas, Temple Fortune, near Golders Green. It was rebuilt completely and much enlarged in 1932, and as late as 1962 a new aisle was added after late repairs caused by bomb damage: however by 1995 this elegant and commodious church, in a prosperous area, was redundant and is now used by Copts.

The first substantial building project in the Diocese of Chelmsford after the First World War was St John, Walthamstow, which is a very large building erected in 1924 after impassioned requests for funds to meet the demands of a newly developed area. In 1961 an extra bay was added together with a permanent west wall to replace temporary arrangements which had been in place since it was built. However as soon thereafter as 1996 it was clear that the accommodation was far too large for the congregation, and the entire interior was rebuilt to substantially reduce the area used for worship.

Although many churches built within the period in question have now been divided internally in the same way, so that extra facilities can be provided and the area needed for worship reduced, it seems that only four permanent buildings from this era have been voluntarily demolished. St Barnabas, erected in 1926 to replace the church blown up in the Silvertown explosion, was knocked down in the 1960s as the area was then depopulated: the locale is now much more fashionable, but no new church has been provided. St Thomas, Acton Vale, which just qualifies for this book on date (1915) was in an area with many other churches: it has been replaced by a block of flats named Canterbury House. Perhaps more importantly, the interesting St John the Divine, Becontree, provided in 1936 by a generous private donor (Mrs Lavinia Keene) has been flattened and replaced by a smaller modern building with none of its presence, and the even later St Matthew, Muswell Hill, a distinguished but understated composition by Caröe & Passmore in 1939, has also gone. As Sir John Betjeman might have said, they were both 'fine churches of unfashionable date'.[2] It looked

for some time that they would be joined by St Cedd, Canning Town, designed by G.G. O'Neill in 1938, which was left empty to deteriorate, but it is now being renovated for further use by the Ghana Seventh Day Adventist Church.

The Second World War saw the destruction of or serious damage to a few churches which had had only a short life, such as St Bede (for the deaf) Clapham, St Catherine Coleman, Hammersmith, and SS. Peter & Paul, Enfield Lock, all the victims of air raids.

There have however been other churches of the era which also enjoyed a much attenuated life for the purpose for which they were intended. The most remarkable of these is almost certainly St Augustine, Wembley Park, designed by the head of the Cambridge University School of Architecture, T.H. Lyon, and dating from 1926. St Augustine's was a striking building which stood high above the semi-detached houses around it: unfortunately the architect had failed to ensure that the foundations were sufficiently deep to bear the weight of that which rested upon them. As early as 1950 the congregation was told to evacuate the church for their own safety after large cracks appeared, and shortly afterwards it had to be demolished before it fell down of its own accord. St Paul, Oxgate (Dollis Hill), by N.F. Cachemaille-Day, which was built in 1939 and is important for his use, for probably the first time, of an almost flat vaulting using exposed concrete construction, was closed in 1980 with scarcely a whimper from the Council for the Care of Churches, and now sees some use as a Hindu temple.

The amount of money available for the building of individual churches varied enormously, even where buildings were erected in adjoining areas of the same development. The vast new Dagenham/Becontree estate, for example, was provided with a variety of church buildings, ranging from the lavish, provided by wealthy donors, such as St John the Divine, Dagenham, which as already mentioned was given by Mrs Lavinia Keene, and St Alban, Becontree, the donation of Dame Violet Wills of the tobacco family, through the medium range of solid but unspectacular churches such as St Elisabeth, Becontree, largely paid for by fund-raising among the Mothers' Union in the Chelmsford Diocese, to temporary buildings such as St Cedd and St Christopher, both in Becontree and both now demolished, and St Peter, also in Becontree, to which a brick built extension was added in 1957 but which is now used as a gospel hall.

There were relatively few instances where the furnishings matched the more ambitious church buildings. St Mary, Kenton, and St Thomas, Hanwell, were two examples where the church was completed as a coherent whole with proper interior fittings, but in most other cases internal work was done piecemeal over a number of years as funds permitted.

The financial issues which overshadowed all new building at this time also led to a number of cases where new churches were financed by the sale of the site of redundant churches in Central London and elsewhere. At one end of the scale was the demolition of the fine Victorian St Andrew, Wells Street and its subsequent rebuilding to the same design and using the same materials and fitments as St Andrew, Kingsbury, under the superintendence of W.A. Forsyth.

Perhaps one of the most unusual churches in London is St Barnabas, Eltham. This started life as a Victorian building by Sir George Gilbert Scott in Woolwich Dockyard. By 1933 it was redundant, but there was a pressing need for a church in the Well Hall area. It was therefore dismantled and removed to Rochester Way, under the direction of T.F. Ford, who also designed a number of new churches in this period and who had, perhaps coincidentally, also once worked for Forsyth. In 1944 however it was gutted, and it was not reopened until 1956-7, by which time Ford's practice had completely reconstructed the interior in a neo-Classical style which, although successful, is quite out of keeping either with the exterior or with the neighbourhood.

St Mary, Kenton was partly paid for by the sale of St Mary, Charing Cross Road, and inherited its strong Anglo-Catholic tradition. St Anselm, Belmont, Harrow, was funded from the former St Anselm, Davies Street, where as it happened the architect of the new church, Cachemaille-Day, had previously worshipped, and there were other such examples.

This process was not confined to Victorian churches which were no longer required. St Olave, Mitcham, took its unusual dedication from a redundant church of the same name in Southwark, which was of mediaeval origin but had been reconstructed on several occasions thereafter. St Catherine Coleman, Hammersmith, took its name and endowments from a former City church and, perhaps most strikingly of all, the Wren tower of All Hallows, Lombard Street, also in the City, was taken down and placed on the Chertsey Road, where it formed part of the new All Hallows, Twickenham. The main part of the new church, which adjoined the tower, was in a contemporary idiom which in fact is not too incongruous and many fittings from the City church were also placed in it.

Middlesex provided particular difficulties for a rapidly expanding population, for in some of the old settlements there were small churches of considerable architectural merit which were quite inadequate for the influx of newcomers. This problem was solved in different ways. At Perivale and Kingsbury the old church was superceded by a new or transplanted building respectively and was made redundant. At Greenford, where the parish rapidly became among the most populous in the Diocese of London, the tiny old church was initially kept in use but was supplemented by a number of daughter churches, which in due course

John Keble Church, Mill Hill (1936) by D.F. Martin-Smith.

were hived off in order to form parishes of their own. A plan was then devised to incorporate the old building into a much larger new church, but in the event the new church, to a design by the distinguished Sir Albert Richardson, was built as a separate entity but very close to its predecessor, which has continued in use for less-well attended services. In Kent, the new church of St Michael, East Wickham, was also built adjacent to the old, which was used for a variety of purposes before being made redundant in 1971.

The variety which has been described was also reflected in the location of the churches which were built. On the St Helier Estate, built by the LCC in what was then Surrey, St Peter, the larger church provided, has a prominent main road site which made it readily visible to all. On the other hand, Bishop Andrewes Church, which was designed to serve the southern part of the new housing, although it was built to an original and not unpleasant design by Geddes Hyslop, is hidden among the back streets and does not even stand up far above them. Holy Cross, Hornchurch, has a prominent corner site on a through road with a large area of well-maintained grass around it which sets off the building and makes the casual passer-by notice it. On the far side of London from that church, St Augustine, Tooting, by the distinguished architect H.P. Burke-Downing and built in his usual refined Gothic Revival style, is hidden up a side street and has to be sought out.

Churchmanship

The growth of new churches must also be seen against the changes in churchmanship which occurred during this period. Winnington-Ingram's benign attitude, and the lack of effective disciplinary machinery, made more acute by the severe blow to the authority of the episcopate generally which resulted from the debacles over the rejection by Parliament in both 1927 and 1928 of the proposals to revise the 1662 Prayer Book, left a power vacuum which was exploited by an Anglo-Catholic Movement emboldened by the success of the Congresses held between 1920 and 1933. Winnington-Ingram's lack of 'discipline' in the Diocese was legendary. That lack of central direction was certainly not present in Southwark during Garbett's time and that efficiency would no doubt have been translated northwards to London had Garbett succeeded in his long-held ambition to follow Ingram in that see. The Dioceses of Chelmsford and Rochester too did not allow the outer edges of the Catholic Movement to flourish with the freedom found in London.

In any event, the inter-war period did not manifest

St Saviour, Eltham (1932): pulpit, by Cachemaille-Day.

in the suburbs as clear a move towards Catholic practices as was evident in the inner city areas. That statement requires some qualification, in that of course there were some new churches, such as Holy Cross, Greenford, and St Mary, Kenton, where Anglo-Catholic worship took root from the very beginning. In others, such as St Patrick, Wallington, and St George, Morden, the Evangelical tradition of the neighbourhood continued in the new foundations. In many more however, what could be seen was a moderate, perhaps debased, English Use with two rather than six candlesticks on the high altar and a degree of ceremonial which would have been regarded as daring in 1900 but by 1930 was well behind the bastions of the Full Faith in the East End and elsewhere. The Liturgical Movement had made very little progress before the war and even the most apparently daring modernist church within this period, St Saviour, Eltham, was in fact built for traditional worship, with a long nave and a sanctuary at the east end with a lady chapel on the north side. There were one or two nods towards the future, such as the altar under the central tower in St Francis of Assisi, Gladstone Park, but they were rare. Congregational participation was not regarded as important: even the well-known scheme for the repositioning of the choir among the people at John Keble Church, Mill Hill, did not affect the relationship between priest and worshippers.

Architects and their designs: traditional or modern?

It is often said that the period between the wars, particularly perhaps the 1930s, represents in architectural terms a battle between the traditionalists and the modernists. As with many generalisations, that contains a modicum of truth. However, when one looks at the churches which were actually built in London during the period in question, it is clear that any such battle was won quite decisively by the traditionalists. It is very easy to obtain a distorted view of the nature of new building in any particular age by concentrating only on a few prominent or interesting buildings. If the whole corpus of churches erected in London between 1915 and 1945 is examined more closely it is clear beyond peradventure that the vast majority of them were traditional in both design and execution. The same is true even of the

decade from 1930 to 1939 during which the ideas of the Modern Movement were gaining ground.

There was no central control over the designs used. The general procedure was that the design emerged locally and often depended on the predilections of the vicar or sometimes of a rich benefactor who was willing to help. The relevant Diocesan Advisory Committee then had to accept or reject the proposals and then, if the new building was to be a parish church, it had also to be approved at both planning and completion stages by the Ecclesiastical Commissioners, whose consulting architects, Caröe and Passmore, were themselves prominent in the field of designing new churches. However the role of the Commissioners in this field was not aesthetically based but rather practical and they therefore afforded a filter against designs which would not work as opposed to designs which were daring in their conception.

In the first part of the period with which we are concerned, the First World War years, a small number of projects which had been started before 1914 were completed, but there was no discernable difference between the churches built during those years and those which immediately preceded them. St Catherine, Neasden, of 1917 by J.S. Alder (then very near the end of his life) is indistinguishable from many other Edwardian Gothic churches, and the same is true of St Luke, Ilford, by E.T. Dunn (1915), and St Paul, Goodmayes, where extensive work was done to 1917 in taking forward a building started some years before by Chancellor & Son. There were however signs even at that time that there was a move towards a basilica design in new churches, such as St Peter, Acton Green (1915) by W.A. Pite, and St Augustine, Belvedere (1916) by W.H. Wood. Perhaps the grandest of the new churches of those war years is St James, Riddlesdown (previously known as St James, Coulsdon) (1915), by Greenaway & Newberry, in a refined and ageless neo-Gothic.

St Augustine, Belvedere (1915), by W.H. Wood, baldachino.

in the East, with the first church on the Dagenham estate (St Thomas, Becontree) being opened in 1926 and others following in rapid succession over the next ten years. By the 1930s streets of suburban villas were covering acres of land all around London, but especially in Middlesex, and the churches followed as soon as money permitted.

The two most prolific ecclesiastical architects on the traditional wing throughout the whole of this period were the Newberry partnerships and Sir Charles Nicholson. J.E. Newberry (1862-1950) was in partnership with F.H. Greenaway (1869-1935) from 1904 until 1926 when the latter retired. He was then in partnership with C.W. Fowler from 1927 until 1945, when he retired but Fowler continued in practice. The successive firms of Greenaway & Newberry and Newberry & Fowler produced a large number of sound, well-designed, careful churches for the suburbs, usually in red brick. Their neo-Gothic idiom is not surprising, bearing in mind that Greenaway had been articled to the Arts and Crafts-influenced Sir Aston Webb, but, perhaps more importantly, Newberry had worked for both James Brooks and then John Loughborough Pearson. The training he received from these two master architects of the nineteenth-century Gothic Revival is well shown in the churches with which he was concerned in the interwar period.

The safe, conservative work of the Newberry partnerships typifies ecclesiastical work in the 1915-45 period much better than does the originality of Cachemaille-Day or the occasional forays into church-building of very distinguished and established architects such as Sir Herbert Baker and Sir Albert Richardson. If there is an archetypal church of the period, then St Martin, Dagenham (1932) by Newberry & Fowler will serve as well as any. As already set out, the churches for the new Dagenham conurbation were of a great variety of specifications and styles. St Martin falls in

There was a lull immediately after the end of the First World War as the country recovered from the enormous expenditure which had been involved, and the consequent economic problems. The pace of new building in London began to accelerate after about 1925, especially in South London, where it was estimated that the shift of population within the Diocese of Southwark alone was to involve 300,000 people. The expansion south of the Thames was followed by that

St Michael and All Angels, Gidea Park (1938) by J. J. Crowe.

the middle: in other words it was neither a temporary building nor one of the lavish, privately donated, now over-large permanent churches. A red-brick building which would fit comfortably into any urban scene, it now looks perfectly at place in its setting.

The other architect whose work perhaps typifies the years in question is the far better known Sir Charles Nicholson (1867-1949). He too had close connections to Arts & Crafts traditions: he was articled to John Dando Sedding and then worked as assistant to Sedding's successor Henry Wilson. Nicholson's practice was enormous, and he was for various periods consultant architect to seven cathedrals and Diocesan architect to four dioceses, including Chelmsford.

Although his father had been given a baronetcy for political services in Australia, the family in fact came from Benfleet, in south-east Essex, and Nicholson lived for a time in Southend, where he restored Porters, now the Civic House, and built a number of churches. Peter Anson's comments on him are well known but worth repeating:

> Sir Charles Nicholson … became the really representative Anglican architect of the first three decades of the [twentieth] century. He designed furnishings which were both traditional and refined. The faint period flavour about them was inoffensive and the use of colour was in keeping with contemporary 'good taste'. A church designed and furnished by Sir Charles always provided the right background for the services of the *Book of Common Prayer*, carried out with loyal but rich Catholic ceremonial. None of his churches show a Papalist influence … A typical Charles Nicholson interior reflects the spirit of the Caroline Divines.[3]

In particular, Nicholson was a devotee of the so-called 'English altar' with riddle posts, as originally championed by Comper before he moved into his inclusive period. Comper built no new church in London in this period, although he added furnishings and stained glass to many.

The Downham estate in South London was not as large an undertaking as was Dagenham in the East, but it too required a number of new churches. Garbett, influenced by his own experience of the Portsea system of organisation using a central church with a number of smaller dependent churches around it, set up a similar method of working in the new area. Unlike Dagenham also, with its variety both of buildings and of architects, Nicholson designed all the new buildings in that area: St Barnabas and St Luke in Downham itself, St Dunstan, Bellingham, St John the Baptist, Southend, and also the nearby St Andrew, Bromley. A similar attempt by Garbett to organise St Helier foundered on the rock of obstinacy provided by Evangelical interests in the parish of Morden, but did result in another commission for the architect in the large church of St Peter.

Nicholson's churches are more ingenious than those of Newberry and his partners, and less tied to stylistic precedents, often incorporating ideas from Classical and Byzantine models, but almost always with a powerful use of space. His work has similarities to that of J. Harold Gibbons, who equally succeeded in adapting new materials to older forms, and also used space to good advantage, which he may well have learnt from a short period as assistant to Temple Moore, the prolific neo-Gothic architect of the late Victorian and Edwardian years. Gibbons' St Mary, Kenton, is one of the outstanding churches of the period, not least because money was not as short there as was the case elsewhere.

Temple Moore also influenced J.J. Crowe, who was at one time his clerk of works. Crowe built St Michael, Gidea Park, and the nearby St Peter, Harold Wood and rebuilt the church of the adjoining parish of All Saints, Squirrells Heath, employing traditional forms.

Cyril Farey was another architect who was able to take forward traditional idioms, often employing a central tower as a focus of his designs, which have lasted well. His commissions came towards the end of the period, and two, All Hallows, North Greenford, and St Peter, Grange Park, post-dated the outbreak of the Second World War: indeed the latter used materials salvaged from other churches which had already been wrecked by air raids.

Other more traditionally minded designers continued to find clients. H.P. Burke-Downing always succeeded in reproducing in his refined, academic Gothic the better churches of the Victorians, although by 1931 (All Saints, Hackbridge) his style was something of an anachronism. C.G. Hare was another somewhat backward looking architect, carrying forward the ideas of Bodley, whose practice he took over, into the post 1918 era with a substantial rebuilding of St Benet & All Saints, Kentish Town (1928), and the construction of St Mildred, Addiscombe (1931), which was unfinished when he died.

William Douglas Caröe (1857-1938), later in partnership with Herbert Passmore (1868-1966), was, apart from his work with the Commissioners, also himself involved in designing churches using a variety of styles: St Michael & All Angels, Mill Hill (1922) is Gothic, but St John the Divine, Romford (1927), and St Oswald, Norbury (1934), both show influences from a wide variety of sources. Caröe is one of the few architectural figures prominent in this period to be the subject of a full study.[4]

Apart from Caröe, there were a number of other very distinguished figures in the architectural establishment who featured on the ecclesiastical scene. Sir Herbert Baker (1862-1946) had worked extensively in South Africa, where he designed the Parliament Buildings in Pretoria, and India, where he collaborated with Lutyens in the planning of New Delhi: he then worked extensively for the War Graves Commission. He returned to London in 1913 and his commission for St Andrew, Ilford (1923), may be thought by some to pale into insignificance beside his other public work. However it is a stately church which has lasted well and is superior to almost every other new church built in Essex in London during the period.

Sir Giles Gilbert Scott (1880-1960) was not only a scion of the most famous architectural dynasty of the day, but had also been awarded the commission for the Anglican cathedral in Liverpool at the young age of 23. He again designed only one church in London during the period, St Alban, Golders Green (1933), which was said by some to offer a synthesis of traditional and modern approaches to church building, utilising a cross shaped plan.

Sir Albert Richardson (1880-1964) had been an assistant both to Evelyn Hellicar, who himself designed St John the Evangelist, Welling, of the churches featured in this book, and to the well-known architect of Roman Catholic churches, Leonard Stokes. His timber-framed Holy Cross, Greenford, was built under special licence because the war had broken out just as work began. The church has been much praised as timeless by some, but has not been improved by its subsequent internal reordering and now looks somewhat tired.

The use of timber was not unique to Greenford: in 1929 the 'Barn Church', St Philip & All Saints, Kew, was recreated literally from a redundant barn. It was followed almost immediately by another such conversion, also under the auspices of E.A. Swan, at St Alban, Sutton. Both these perhaps reflect the final flowering of the Arts and Crafts Movement: St Alban was built in the mediaeval fashion without modern scaffolding being used and both reflect a somewhat self-conscious rejection of modern techniques and ideas.

W. Curtis Green (1875-1960) was best known for his exquisite draughtsmanship, but he designed one church within the parameters of this book, St George, Waddon, in 1932: the pleasing design is equalled only by the difficulty in finding the building in a maze of narrow one-way streets.

S.D. Adshead (1868-1946) was the first professor of Town Planning, being elected to a chair at Liverpool before the First World War. Among his commissions was the redevelopment of the Duchy of Cornwall's estate at Kennington, which was an early example of neo-Georgian work.[5] From that came the commission for St Anselm, Kennington Cross, unique for the period in its proximity to Central London, which was planned before that War but not completed until 1932, and then to revised designs. It is a stately basilica of Early Christian inspiration and at least survives in an area where many churches have been closed and demolished.

St George, Waddon (1932) by W. Curtis Green.

being beautifully maintained and presented and the rare distinction of generally being open to visit.

Just as Maufe is best known in ecclesiastical circles for his work at Guildford, Milner and Craze are associated in the minds of many, especially those of a specific altitude in their churchmanship, with Walsingham. Sir William Milner, Bart, was a great friend of Father Hope Patten, the refounder of the Shrine of Our Lady of Walsingham, and was one of the original Guardians. He was personally a great benefactor of the work at Walsingham, and his partner, Romilly Craze, designed the shrine buildings. However the practice, originally Milner Craze & Urquhart, and later simply Milner & Craze, designed a wide variety of churches in different styles. In the new East London developments, they built both St Alban, Becontree (1934), a very substantial neo-Gothic work, and the nearby St George, Dagenham (1935), which was constructed to a very tight budget, which is reflected in its appearance and interior.

The partnership of the Hon. John Seely (later Lord Mottistone) and Paul Paget was considerably more modernist in its attitude towards design, and they were not afraid to use unconventional ideas: sometimes these did not bear fruit, as with the rather odd St John the Baptist, Tottenham, which fails to make use of its prominent position, but on other occasions the total effect is much more pleasing, as at The Ascension, Hanger Hill, where fine use is made of curved lines.

Anson calls Welch, Cachemaille-Day and Lander 'the most revolutionary ecclesiastical architects during this period'.[6] In fact, the partnership between the three of them had a short life, being formed about 1929 and being dissolved in 1935. Although Herbert Welch (1883-1953) and Felix Lander (1898-1960) continued in practice thereafter, building the mission church of St Martin, East Barnet in 1938, they did not specialise in the ecclesiastical market, which was the main interest of Cachemaille-Day.

The best-known ecclesiastical work of Sir Edward Maufe (1883-1974) is of course Guildford Cathedral. However his distinctive style, timeless but drawing on earlier precedents, had been seen before that in London, firstly in his two churches for the deaf, St Bede, Clapham, and St Saviour, Acton (both 1924), but more importantly in his masterly St Thomas, Hanwell (1934), which has many echoes of Guildford. If St Martin, Dagenham, is the most typical church of its era, St Thomas, Hanwell, is perhaps the outstanding such building of the period. It also has the benefit of

All Hallows, North Greenford (1941) by Cyril Farey.

Nugent Francis Cachemaille-Day (1896-1976) had worked in the development of Welwyn Garden City and then as chief assistant to H.S. Goodhart-Rendel, who is as well known for his written output as for his architecture, and whose knowledge of Victorian architects was not only profound but well ahead of his time.

Cachemaille-Day won the RIBA London Architecture Medal for St Saviour, Eltham (1932), completed while he was still in the partnership. The church was strongly influenced by contemporary work in Germany and Holland, and while it is extremely widely known it is quite unrepresentative of other churches being erected in London at the time and, incidentally, nothing like as revolutionary in concept as the architect's contemporary church of St Michael & All Angels, Wythenshawe, Manchester. Another church by Cachemaille-Day, St Mary, Becontree, is less well known but is original in both design and use of materials. St Paul, South Harrow, also by him, is certainly unusual in its conception but few would call its cinema-like appearance attractive. The same could be said of the extraordinary St Patrick, Barking, designed by A.E. Wiseman, which from a distance resembles a tube station.

However even Cachemaille-Day was, at the same time as he designed these novel places of worship, also building churches which were far more traditional both in concept and in execution, although always with his novel and careful approach to detail, such as St Edmund, South Chingford, and St Laurence, Barkingside, and at St Edward, Perivale Park, he produced a small and conventional hall/church rather similar to many being built under the auspices of the Forty-Five Churches Fund. His total output produced probably the most interesting selection of churches in the area by one individual over this period, but there were a few others who were prepared to move outside the conventional. One was A.W. Kenyon, who also drew on German precedents in his St Alban, North Harrow (1938), a design which has perhaps not dated as well as some, and another was D.F. Martin-Smith, with his much praised John Keble Church, Mill Hill (1936), which survives in a remarkably original state but now has an aura of timelessness about it, which perhaps shows that the early praise lavished upon it was not misplaced.

It was Goodhart-Rendel who famously coined the expression 'rogue architects' to describe certain Victorian designers who did not conform to the norms of the time. It may be applied by analogy to two designers who featured in London ecclesiastical building between the wars, namely Ernest Shearman and Martin Travers. By coincidence one of the authors has studied Shearman's work in detail, the other Travers'.[7]

Ernest Charles Shearman (1859-1939) had a varied career which included a period from 1888 to 1891 in Argentina as architect to the Buenos Aires Great Southern Railway. In 1902 he returned to England. His output of church designs was small, but almost entirely concentrated in and around London. Before 1914 he had designed St Matthew, Wimbledon (destroyed in the Second World War) and St Silas the Martyr, Kentish Town. At the beginning of the First World War he worked on St Barnabas, North Ealing, although as a result of various untoward matters he was dismissed as architect before the building was complete. There was then a considerable gap in his output, before he produced in quick succession St Gabriel, Acton (1929), St Barnabas, Temple Fortune (1932), and then St Francis of Assisi, Isleworth (1933). The latter was a particularly important commission as its location, on the Great West Road out of London, ensured that it was seen by many driving by, whereas all his other churches were in side streets. Shearman's buildings are in a derivation of Mediterranean Gothic, with a somewhat dark and haunting quality which repels some but fascinates others. They are a world away from the use by other architects at this time of Perpendicular forms, flooding the interiors with light. All his churches have similarities, but all repay careful study for the excellence of the design and the intricacy of the rose windows which were a characteristic of Shearman.

Howard Martin Otho Travers (1886-1948) was primarily a stained glass painter and church furnisher, whose exquisite work can be seen enhancing the quality of many churches across the country. He is best known as an exponent of the so-called 'Back to Baroque' Movement, an attempt by some Anglo-Catholics to furnish Anglican churches as if the Reformation had never happened, and his work in that genre on the interiors of St Mary, Bourne Street, Pimlico, and St Magnus the Martyr in the City, is widely praised. Later he designed the enormous reredos for St Augustine, Queen's Gate, South Kensington, in the style of Spain or South America but using modern motifs as well. However Travers had no firm religious beliefs himself and it is wrong to imagine that his appeal was confined to that small section of the Church of England.

Travers was not a member of the RIBA. In the late 1920s and early 1930s he decided to move towards the construction of complete churches, which in certain cases meant that he had to collaborate with a registered architect in order that his designs be accepted. He worked with T.F.W. Grant, who translated Travers' sketches into working drawings and in fact had a considerable ecclesiastical practice of his own, mainly in Kent. The attempt was not ultimately very successful, but it did lead to the construction of three unusual and interesting churches in this area: Good Shepherd, Carshalton Beeches (1930), Holy Redeemer, Streatham Vale (1932), and Emmanuel, Leyton (1936). All of these make use of Baroque forms, although only the former was for a church where Anglo-Catholicism was established and the other two were for definitely Evangelical congregations.

Using this book

The main part of this book is a gazetteer arranged by area. The churches have been set out under the London borough where they stand as it is hoped this will be the most readily comprehensible form of organisation.

References are given at the end of each entry to the main published sources (see Abbreviations p. 26).

It was also thought that it would be helpful to list the architects and firms with a cross-reference to the churches which they designed, and this follows the gazetteer.

Notes

1. See S.C. Carpenter, *Winnington-Ingram* (Hodder & Stoughton, 1949), pp. 186-7.
2. See J. Betjeman, *Collins Pocket Guide to English Parish Churches,* various editions, dedication.
3. P.F. Anson, *Fashions in Church Furnishings 1840-1940* (Studio Vista, 1965), pp. 347-8.
4. See J.M. Freeman, *W.D. Caröe RStO FSA: His Architectural Achievement* (Manchester University Press, 1990). She tells us that his name, of Danish origin, is pronounced to rhyme with Harrow.
5. See C.H. Reilly, *Representative British Architects of the Present Day* (Batsford, 1931), pp. 15-28.
6. Anson [note 3], p. 343.
7. John Salmon's researches on Shearman are unpublished but have been drawn upon in this book: see also Rodney Warrener & Michael Yelton, *Martin Travers (1886-1948): an Appreciation* (Unicorn Press, 2003).

GAZETTEER

ABBREVIATIONS

FMC   *Fifty Modern Churches* (Incorporated Church Building Society, 1947).

NCI   *New Churches Illustrated* (Incorporated Church Building Society, 1936).

Pevsner, 2   Bridget Cherry & Nikolaus Pevsner, *The Buildings of England: London 2: South* (Penguin, 1983).

Pevsner, 3   Bridget Cherry & Nikolaus Pevsner, *The Buildings of England: London 3: North West* (Penguin, 1991).

Pevsner, 4   Bridget Cherry & Nikolaus Pevsner, *The Buildings of England: London 4: North* (Penguin, 1998).

Pevsner, 5   Bridget Cherry, Charles O'Brien & Nikolaus Pevsner, *The Buildings of England: London 5: East* (Yale University Press, 2005).

Richardson   Kenneth Richardson, *The 'Twenty-Five' Churches of the Southwark Diocese: an Inter-War Campaign of Church-building* (Ecclesiological Society, 2002).

VCHE, 5   W.R. Powell (ed.), *A History of the County of Essex: Volume V* (OUP, 1966).

VCHE, 6   W.R. Powell (ed.), *A History of the County of Essex: Volume VI* (OUP, 1973).

VCHE, 7   W.R. Powell (ed.), *A History of the County of Essex: Volume VII* (OUP, 1978).

VCHM, 3   Susan Reynolds (ed.), *A History of the County of Middlesex: Volume III* (OUP, 1962).

VCHM, 4   J.S. Cockburn & T.F.T. Baker (eds), *A History of the County of Middlesex: Volume IV* (OUP, 1971).

VCHM, 5   T.F.T. Baker (ed.) *A History of the County of Middlesex: Volume V* (OUP, 1976).

VCHM, 6   T.F.T. Baker (ed.), *A History of the County of Middlesex: Volume VI* (OUP, 1980).

VCHM, 7   T.F.T. Baker (ed.), *A History of the County of Middlesex: Volume VII* (OUP, 1982).

BARKING & DAGENHAM

St Alban, Becontree

Status: in use.
Location: corner of Vincent and Urswick Roads.
Nearest station: Becontree.
Constructed: 1934.
Architects: Milner & Craze.

There could scarcely be a greater contrast between a church and its surroundings than is provided by St Alban, Becontree. In a maze of side streets, all provided with the cottage style houses erected by the LCC, stands this handsome, expensive church built of large stone blocks, with one of the few towers that were actually constructed, as opposed to planned, for ecclesiastical buildings of the interwar era. The money for this fine building was provided by Dame Violet Wills of the tobacco family, and for her £14,000 the architects

delivered a very substantial neo-Perpendicular church. The tower dwarfs the surrounding housing and provides a landmark on the very flat area on which the estate was built. The nave is aisleless and of great length, not only absolutely but also in proportion to the tower. The nave windows are clear save for strange Art Deco-influenced leading. While they are neo-Perpendicular, the large east window, which has painted glass in it, is nearer to Decorated. The altar has a stone reredos with corner posts and even the early photographs do not show side curtains. The font is of stone, the roof of wood, the trusses of which run low down the nave walls. The tradition is Evangelical and the interior is bare. This is one of the churches which is now far too large for its congregation, but the ambition which built it should be given appropriate respect.

References: Pevsner, 5, p. 141; VCHE, 5, p. 244.

St Cedd, Becontree

Status: demolished and replaced.
Former Location: Lodge Avenue, east side, north of junction with Bromhall Road.
Constructed: 1936.
Architect: not known.

St Cedd was a temporary church which seems to have been camera shy. In 1963 it was demolished and replaced by a modern church of the same name on an adjoining site: although the tradition was Evangelical, the foundation stone of the new building was laid by local MP Tom Driberg, a prominent Anglo-Catholic.

Reference: VCHE, 5, p. 245.

St Christopher, Becontree

Status: demolished.
Former Location: Raydons Road.
Constructed: 1931.
Architect: E. Meredith.

St Christopher was another of the temporary churches erected as the Becontree area developed. It was built on a site which was intended for the permanent church of St Elisabeth (q.v.), but in the event that was erected at a much more prominent position, although St Christopher was retained, initially as a mission church for children. It was closed about 1962 and then demolished.

Reference: VCHE, 5, p. 244.

St Elisabeth, Becontree

Status: in use.
Location: Wood Lane, corner with Hewett Road.
Nearest station: Becontree.
Constructed: 1932.
Architect: Sir Charles Nicholson.

While St Alban contrasts with its surroundings, the red brick used by Nicholson for St Elisabeth is in harmony with the adjoining houses. This church was built with funds subscribed by the branches of the Mothers' Union over the Diocese of Chelmsford, and was originally to have been dedicated to St Mary, as the patron saint of the Union. However, at the laying of the foundation stone on 23rd May 1931 by the then Duchess of York, the diocesan president of the MU, Mrs

dedication was changed. The church itself was a classic design by Nicholson: understated, always competent, and combining seamlessly both Gothic and classical elements. The exterior is neo-Jacobean, with large late Gothic windows at the east and west ends, but aisles on both sides with square-headed windows. Inside, however, there are classical columns with round arches resting on them, and a barrel roof. There is no tower, but a small bell cote which stands above the northern entrance door. The sanctuary now has a curtain behind the altar, which has been pulled out in the current way. The tradition is moderate. An adjoining hall did not, as was usually the case, precede the church, but was built simultaneously and opened the same year.

References: Pevsner, 5, p. 141; VCHE, 5, p. 244.

L.H. Inskip, wife of the Bishop of Barking, announced that it was to be dedicated to St Elizabeth in honour of the royal visitor, who is recorded in the contemporary press as wearing her trademark powder blue which was to become so familiar in later years when she had become the Queen Mother. Later the spelling of the

St Erkenwald, Barking

Status: in use as hall to main church.
Location: Levett Road, south side, near Upney Lane junction.
Nearest station: Upney.
Constructed: 1934.
Architect: not known.

This brick built hall was constructed in order to serve as a temporary church for a new Peel district within the ancient parish of St Margaret, Barking. It was used until the building of a new church immediately in front of it, in 1954. It then became the parish hall, although in 2004 it reverted to use as a church during works to the new church, which have now been completed.

References: Pevsner, 5, p, 124; VCHE, 5, p. 244.

St George, Dagenham

Status: in use.
Location: Rogers Road, opposite junction with Pettits Road.
Nearest station: Dagenham Heathway.
Constructed: 1935.
Architects: Milner & Craze.

This church (sometimes called St George, Becontree) is another contrast with St Alban, Becontree, particularly since it was designed by the same firm. Whereas St

Alban had a private donor, this building was constructed to a tight budget and the result is an undemonstrative low yellow brick basilica now nearly hidden from the road by the trees which have grown since the pictures of it when new in *Fifty Modern Churches*. There are a few flourishes, including a small bell-tower in Italian style and a cross in brick on the exterior of the east wall, which however now looks out on to houses and a fence. The interior is bare brick even in the narrow chancel, and the altar has simple hangings behind, which have been extended over the years so that they now reach over the whole east end. The windows are

small and oblong and the piers to the arcades on north and south are square and plain. The roof is timber and in the nave the trusses are carried down to just above the openings to the arcade and supported on stone corbels. The tradition is central. Although the specification was frugal, the church is probably better suited to the needs of the twenty-first century than some of its more distinguished neighbours. It appears to have succeeded a temporary building of 1929.

References: Pevsner, 5, p. 142; VCHE, 5, p. 297; FMC, p. 112.

St John the Divine, Becontree

Status: demolished and replaced.
Former Location: Goresbrook Road, north side, near junction with Canonsleigh Road.
Constructed: 1936.
Architect: A.E. Wiseman.

St John the Divine was a substantial church to an original design by A.E. Wiseman (1893-1953) of Chelmsford,

made possible by the munificence of Mrs Lavinia Keene of Galleywood, who later donated the money for St Patrick, Barking, by the same architect. It replaced an earlier temporary building. The permanent church was in memory of the donor's husband and named after him, and cost about £10,000. It was demolished after a life of only some 50 years and replaced by a small and undistinguished building on an adjoining site, one of the first permanent churches of its era to suffer that fate. Wiseman built in red brick, which suited the neighbourhood, and produced a Byzantine basilica with a square tower placed over an entrance half way along the south side and a lady chapel. The windows were arched. Even Pevsner, in 1964, was forced to a grudging admission that the interior was 'remarkable', with a substantial tunnel vault, seven arches separating the nave

St Martin, Dagenham

Status: in use.
Location: Goresbrook Road, south side, near junction with Ripple Road.
Nearest station: Dagenham Heathway.
Constructed: 1932.
Architects: Newberry & Fowler.

It is entirely appropriate that Newberry & Fowler should produce an archetypical 1930s church in one of the archetypical settings for such a church, near a parade of shops in Dagenham. It replaced a temporary church of 1925. The church is externally of red brick with a small flèche between chancel and nave rather than a full blown spire, a roof which takes in aisles on both sides as well as the nave and chancel, and neo-Perpendicular windows such as can be found in many other churches by the same architects. There is a particularly fine west window, but at the east end the proximity of the church to other buildings meant that a rose window high above the altar was provided. Martin Travers produced a design at the time for a Christ in Glory in the rose window and a reredos in *opus sectile* above the altar

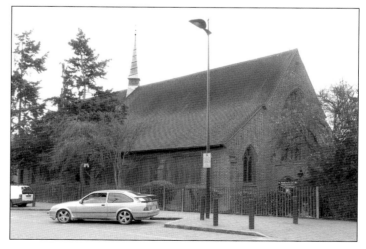

from the side passages, and a triple arch between nave and chancel. The inside walls were cream plaster, and surviving photographs show other interesting features such as a circular marble pulpit with integral staircase around it, and matching font and lectern. The church was complete with vestries and other accoutrements, unlike many of its age which were built to minimum specifications and then added to later. It is a great shame that it has not been saved.

References: Pevsner, Essex, p. 80; VCHE, 5, p. 244.

32

which would have covered much of the space between it and the window, and this was exhibited at the Royal Academy in 1932. Unfortunately the funds were not forthcoming, and the window still has clear glass. In 1949 the east wall was provided with a Crucifixion mural by Hans Feibusch. In contrast to the exterior, the brick of the interior is grey/buff which sets off the restrained furnishings, which show more Anglo-Catholic influence than many local churches, although now it is united with the Evangelical St Alban and St John in the South Becontree team ministry. There are dignified arches between the nave and the aisles on octagonal piers and a wooden roof. The whole ensemble works as well as many more ambitious designs.

References: Pevsner, 5, p.142; VCHE, 5, p. 296; NCI, p.126.

St Mary, Becontree

Status: in use.
Location: Grafton Road, east side, near junction with Valence Wood Road.
Nearest station: Dagenham Heathway.
Constructed: 1935.
Architects: Welch, Cachemaille-Day & Lander.

This extraordinary church is rightly described in the *Buildings of England* as 'distinctive and important'. It is also, in contrast to much of Cachemaille-Day's other work, little known, perhaps because of its location. The striking appearance was even more arresting when the church was first built and it was not as hemmed in as it now is by surrounding buildings. An earlier temporary church built in 1927 was replaced after desperately needed funds for this building became available from the endowments of the former Ram's Chapel in Homerton, together with the organ and communion plate. The most original feature is a large tower over the sanctuary, which has a stair turret on the corner topped by a belfry of eight concrete columns, the whole looking like a stylised castle. The exterior is rendered in cream on brick, and in several places the render has fallen away. The nave and the single north aisle have a somewhat odd appearance because of the steep, separate roofs on each, and the windows and doors are surrounded by black bricks which accentuate them against the render. The west windows of both nave and aisle make use of curved sides which produce a slightly mesmeric effect.

The interior in particular reflects the fact that the living was in the hands of the ultra-Evangelical Church Pastoral Aid Society, with integral lecterns at each end of the wooden altar table, which is however elaborately carved, as are the rails. However, Cachemaille-Day used the characteristic device of lighting the plain sanctuary from above, accentuating also the narrow east window by Christopher Webb. The arches behind the altar are buff brick, but the chancel is rendered white and the roof alternates wooden beams with white render and has substantial arches resting on corbels.

References: Pevsner, 5, p. 142; VCHE, 5, p. 297.

St Patrick, Barking

Status: in use.
Location: Blake Avenue, west side, opposite Denham Way.
Nearest station: Upney.
Constructed: 1940.
Architect: A.E. Wiseman.

This church of St Patrick, Barking, like the demolished St John, Dagenham, was designed by A.E. Wiseman and built by the donation of Mrs Lavinia Keene. The two are, however, very different. One of the most extraordinary features of this peculiar looking building is that it was constructed just after the outbreak of the Second World War, in an area where many churches were bombed, but it survived intact. It replaced a hall known as The Ascension in Tudor Avenue, which then became the parish hall but is now demolished. Mrs Keene spent about £10,500, slightly more than she had expended on the much more lavish Dagenham church. Pevsner described this as 'an odd attempt at modern church architecture.' It is certainly unusual, and possibly unique, in that the Round Tower Church Society consider that this is the only Anglican church with a round tower at the eastern end. It would not be unfair to say that the whole ensemble resembles a warehouse with a circular projection which could easily be taken for the entrance to a Holden underground station. To be entirely fair to the architect, his flèche to top the tower was never erected and it is only a large cross in the brick (picked out in green) and a small cross on the flat roof of the tower which alert the passer by to the true nature of the building. The appearance is not helped by the fact that a subsequent reordering and division of the nave has resulted in some windows being bricked up. The interior is equally remarkable, with a stylised concrete rood beam with cross above, not only anachronistic but out of sympathy with the Evangelicalism of the teaching, and there is more concrete in the piers, which taper towards the floor rather than to the roof. The sanctuary is of course under the tower, which has plaster decoration on its ceiling and east wall which would have graced a suburban Essoldo. On each side of the tower are low transepts with semicircular ends. All in all, this church, hidden away in the back streets, is a draw for the connoisseur of the unlikely.

References: Pevsner, 5, p.124; VCHE, 5, p. 244.

St Peter, Becontree

Status: in use as Gospel Hall.
Location: Warrington Road, north side, opposite Warrington Square.
Nearest station: Chadwell Heath.
Constructed: 1931.
Architect: E. Meredith.

This church was a temporary building of hall type with many windows along each side. As with many other projects, the false hopes of the post-Second World War years resulted in unnecessary building. In this case J.J. Crowe designed a brick built east end with chancel, lady chapel and small bellcote, but in 1997 this church was made redundant and is now used as a gospel hall.

References: Pevsner, 5, p.143; VCHE, 5, p. 297.

St Thomas, Becontree

Status: in use.
Location: Haydon Road, at junction with Burnside Road.
Nearest station: Chadwell Heath.
Constructed: 1926.
Architects: Blomfield & Driver.

This church was the first built by the Church of England on the Becontree estate, succeeding a temporary building which in turn took the place of a hut known as the 'Ritz canteen'. The part played by the energetic vicar in the development of the social life and institutions of the new community is recorded in the report on the estate prepared for the Pilgrim Trust by Terence Young in 1934, a useful source of information. In 1926 it was possible to erect a permanent church with the aid of funds from the sale of the redundant St Jude, Whitechapel. The Anglicans were particularly anxious to build because the Roman Catholics had erected their own church of St Peter opposite where St Thomas stands, and of course in those days there was no question of sharing premises. The foundation stone was laid on 3rd July 1926 by Mrs J.W. Eisdell, the daughter of the

first Bishop of Barking, and the architects produced a large but unexciting and backward-looking building of red brick. It has turrets on either side of the west front, but no tower, and three substantial gables on each side which produce tall arches along the nave which alternate with lower arches between the gables. There is a lady chapel with its own roof, and the chancel roof is lower than that of the nave, producing a disjunctive effect for a church built at one time. The interior is of brick with an English altar with angels on the posts. In 1985 a reordering reduced the size of the nave by inserting parish rooms, a familiar development.

References: Pevsner, 5, p. 143; VCHE, 5, p. 259.

BARNET

John Keble Church, Mill Hill

Status: in use.
Location: Deans Lane, south side, south of Sefton Avenue.
Nearest station: Mill Hill Broadway.
Constructed: 1936.
Architect: D.F. Martin-Smith.

This is one of the best-known 1930s churches in London and one of the most successful. Remarkably, it is in very much its original condition, although, because of the quality of the design, it has a timeless quality to it and visitors frequently consider it to be more modern than it actually is.

The congregation began worshipping in a wooden hut in 1932 but quickly built a dual-purpose hall/church which, after the construction of the permanent church adjacent to it, reverted to use as the hall. The unusual dedication, perhaps influenced by the imminence of the Oxford Movement centenary, was the brainchild of the Rev. Eric Milner-White, later Dean of York. The construction of the church was influenced by the ideas of the first vicar, the Rev. O.H. Gibbs-Smith which he had already expounded while the hut church was in use: although the sanctuary arrangement is traditional, he was one of the early exponents of Parish Communion, and he devised the novel position for the choir within the main body of the building, surrounded by the congregation. Time has shown the disadvantages of that arrangement, because there is thus a large unused space when a choir is not required and also the choir is a long way from the organ. However it was regarded as revolutionary in placing the choir so that they did not divide the priest from the congregation.

Martin-Smith (whose brother was organist at the church) won the commission in a competition, and his building has been much praised then and now, although it was his first ecclesiastical essay. It is built of reinforced concrete with buff brick around it, at a cost of £13,500. The main body of the church, from the outside, is rectangular and unremarkable, but the west front has a flat-roofed tower with a smaller square tower on it, topped by a lantern of concrete and a cross above all. There are echoes of Scandinavia in the design. Inside, Martin-Smith used diagonal coffering to create a 'diagrid' ceiling, the first time this had been used in an English church: the panels are coloured and contrast with the cool white of the walls. There is abstract stained glass on the east wall: the chancel is wide but very shallow, an arrangement which means that no separate nave altar is required to fulfil modern liturgical ideas. It was possible simply to move the altar forward a short distance, while retaining its relationship to the building. There are many arresting details in the original fittings, including lights, all designed by the architect. Above the altar is a mosaic panel showing the Holy Spirit in blue and gold by A.F. Erridge, a verger at the church who had artistic talents. The vicarage, also designed by Martin-Smith, was added in 1952. This church well repays a visit.

References: Pevsner, 4, p. 156; VCHM, 5, p. 37; NCI, p. 156; FMC, p. 34.

St Alban, Golders Green

Status: in use.
Location: North End Road, corner of West Heath Drive.
Nearest station: Golders Green.
Constructed: 1933.
Architect: Sir Giles Gilbert Scott.

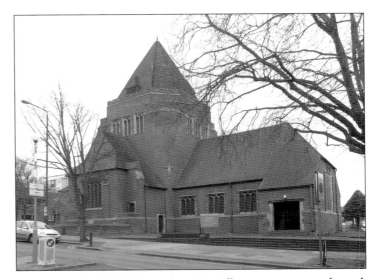

In 1909 a hall dedicated to St Alban was erected, and in 1923 a new parish established. The Rev. H. Trundle, missioner, then first vicar, set up a building fund as early as 1911, but progress was slow until Scott's plans were approved in 1925. Even so it was 1932 before work began: Trundle saw it finished before dying in 1937. Scott's church was of reinforced concrete, hidden from view by the red-brick facings and some stone finishes. The church is relatively small, with a central tower on

the crossing and a modern interpretation of Gothic in the details. The tower has an external turret for a stair to the bell chamber. The tower also lights the area beneath, and that together with the neo-Perpendicular west window ensures that the interior is illuminated from natural sources.

Trundle had stipulated that there should be an unobstructed view of the altar and pulpit, and Scott ensured that that occurred. He himself designed many of the fittings, including the stone reredos, an unusual feature by this time. In due course the congregation absorbed those of St Michael, Golders Green, and St Barnabas, Temple Fortune: an altar and reredos for the lady chapel were transferred from the latter church. Although there have been developments since the church was built, it remains a treasury of Scott design and is relatively little known. It has many furnishings in a moderate Anglo-Catholic idiom which are displayed against white interior walls. It was extensively publicised at the time because it seemed to combine the traditional and the modern.

References: Pevsner, 4, p. 133; VCHM, 5, p. 36; NCI, p. 68.

basilica with narrow passage aisles in what is usually called the Early Christian style, but it was unfinished when consecrated. A planned bell-tower, which would have given the building more interest externally was not built, but in due course, perhaps during restoration from war damage in 1952, a new west end was added with a curious portico above the entrance.

The interior is white and uncluttered. A strong Anglo-Catholic tradition is maintained: Dixon-Spain (1878-1955) was himself a convert to Roman Catholicism and built little for Anglicans. This however is a successful and striking design.

References: Pevsner, 4, p. 157; VCHM, 5, p. 37; NCI, p. 122.

St Alphage, Burnt Oak

Status: in use.
Location: Montrose Avenue, north side, near junction with Burnt Oak Broadway.
Nearest station: Burnt Oak.
Constructed: 1927.
Architects: C. Nicholas & J.E. Dixon-Spain.

The growth of the Watling Estate in the 1920s required a new church, which replaced an earlier mission on a different site. The architects produced a large apsed

St Andrew, Edgware

Status: in use.
Location: Lynford Gardens, at junction with Beulah Close.
Nearest station: Edgware.
Constructed: 1937.
Architect: not known.

A simple brick-built hall/church, nowadays a relatively rare survival. The only unusual feature of this building is that, because of the site plan, the main entrance is on the south side rather than the west as is more common. It is used in the week as a day nursery.

Reference: VCHM, 4, p. 166.

St Barnabas, Temple Fortune

Status: in use by Coptic Church.
Location: Cranbourne Gardens, at junction with Oakfield Road.
Nearest station: Brent Cross.
Constructed: 1932.
Architect: Ernest Shearman.

This is a church with a complicated building history which, despite the money spent on it, had a short life within the Church of England. It has an island site in a prosperous area off main roads. In 1915 J.S. Alder built a temporary hall for what was then called the Holy Name Mission of the London Diocesan Home Mission, and in 1923 it was consecrated as the parish church. In 1932 Shearman added to it very considerably by designing a chancel, lady chapel, and part of a nave, building up to the wall of the temporary church, but not completing a tower which had also been planned. The church was

damaged in the war, but in 1962 R.B. Craze replaced the remaining part of Alder's nave by a new nave which, although it imitates Shearman's design in size and colour, fails by a long way to imitate its confidence and technique. The extended church was however closed in 1995 after an extraordinarily short life, and is now used by Copts.

The Shearman work is his usual Mediterranean Gothic, with a large and well-detailed rose window in the lady chapel: Craze produced a new rose window in the (liturgical) west wall, which suffers by comparison, as

do his tall thin nave windows. The church has a number of original fittings by Shearman. The building is hidden in suburban streets and is, perhaps for that reason, not well known, but despite the architectural curiosities resulting from its history it is externally very powerful.

References: Pevsner, 4, p. 135; VCHM, 5, p. 37.

St Martin, East Barnet

Status: in use for secular purposes, as community hall.
Location: Brookside East, almost opposite junction with Monkfrith Way.
Nearest station: East Barnet.
Constructed: 1938.
Architects: Welch & Lander.

This angular mission church was in use for only a short time, before being sold in about 1964 for other use. Having been a synagogue at one point, it is now a club. The picture in *Fifty Modern Churches* does not identify it, but at that time it was readily visible from the road: now it is almost entirely surrounded by trees. The architects did not adopt the usual straightforward

brick pattern for a mission, perhaps because of the very hilly site on which the building was constructed, but instead devised their own scheme, which in fact looks more comfortable as a community hall.

Reference: FMC, p. 146.

St Mary Magdalene, Hendon

Status: demolished.
Former location: Holders Hill Road, west side, corner of Foreland Court.
Constructed: 1934.
Architect: not known.

This was a mission church of St Mary, Hendon. It was a wooden building of the type sometimes called a 'hut church', but, unlike many such, it remained in use for very many years. It was low and unpretentious with a tiled roof and domestic-looking windows. It was still in use in the 1970s, but has since been demolished and the site used for other purposes.

Reference: VCHM, 5, p. 37.

St Michael & All Angels, Mill Hill

Status: In use.
Location: Flower Lane, east side, near junction with Mill Hill Broadway.
Nearest station: Mill Hill Broadway.
Constructed: 1922.
Architects: Caröe & Passmore.

This church, like St Barnabas, Temple Fortune, has a complicated building history, but unlike it, is still in

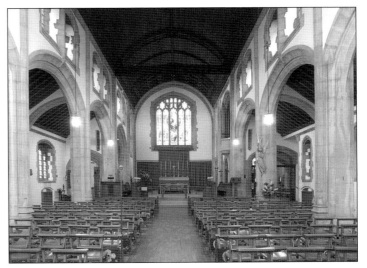

Anglican use. The original plan was devised by Caröe for St Catherine, Gloucester, about 1911 but that project did not proceed and it was used instead for this church. Passmore supervised the first phase of building, in 1921-2 (an unusual period for ecclesiastical development) when the nave was built. The church was extended in 1932 and 1938, completing the east end, but the west end was not finished until 1956, when Alban Caroe modified the earlier designs and also com-

pleted the lady chapel. Despite the long period over which the work was carried out, the result is a coherent, late-Gothic church with many fine details, as is usual with a Caröe design. The large traceried windows at each end are particularly well executed. The tradition is Moderate Catholic, again typical of a Caröe production, but Methodists use the lady chapel on occasion.

References: Pevsner, 4, p. 174; VCHM, 5, p. 37.

CHURCH NOT REQUIRING A FULL ENTRY

St Matthias, Colindale

This hall was built in 1934 and was used as a temporary church until the construction of a new church in modern style behind it in 1971. It is of typical design. The tradition is one of definite Anglo-Catholicism.

BEXLEY

Holy Redeemer, Lamorbey

Status: in use.
Location: Days Lane, corner of Annandale Road.
Nearest station: New Eltham.
Constructed: 1933.
Architect: A.S.R. Ley.

This is an unusual and little-known design by the Kent-based architect Ley (1870-1950). A mission hall was erected in the area in 1909, and then the influx of population after the First World War led to action from

the Bishop of Rochester's Twelve Churches Fund, the equivalent of the better-known campaigns in London and Southwark. It was a pioneering work in that it was built almost entirely of concrete over steel frames. It is set back from the road over an area of green and has a small bell-tower. There is an apse on the east end and rectangular windows on the north and south walls

which are set in brick, although the predominant colour of the walls is white. The entrance has a concrete surround which now looks dated, but was no doubt daring when introduced. The total effect is more striking than the individual parts.

References: none.

St Augustine, Belvedere

Status: in use.
Location: Gilbert Road, corner of St Augustine Road.
Nearest station: Belvedere.
Constructed: 1916.
Architect: W.H. Wood.

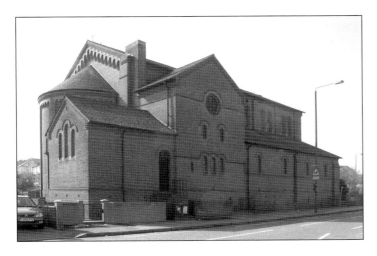

In 1884 a corrugated-iron church was erected on a site now occupied by the vicarage. In 1915 the foundation stone of a new basilica was laid: the North-Eastern

architect W.H. Wood modified plans originally drawn up by his former partner C.H. Fowler, who had died in 1910. When consecrated in 1916 the original west end was wooden, and a new one was not completed until 1962. The church is of red brick and imposing rather than attractive from the exterior. The interior is more satisfying: a large baldachino was erected over the high altar and it has been decorated in accordance with Anglo-Catholic taste: it is now a Forward in Faith church.

Reference: Pevsner, 2, p. 132.

St James the Great, Blendon

Status: in use.
Location: Penhill Road, corner of Bladindon Drive.
Nearest station: Albany Park.
Constructed: 1937.
Architect: not known.

This is an adaptation by the Diocese of Rochester of the simple hall/church, which has remained in use to this day. The only external distinguishing features are a small bell-tower and a cross on the west wall. It is built of red brick. The interior is devoid of any interesting furnishings.

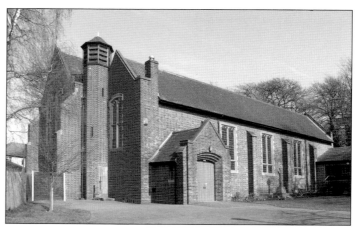

References: none.

St John the Evangelist, Welling

Status: in use.
Location: Roseacre Road, corner of Danson Lane.
Nearest station: Welling.
Constructed: 1926.
Architect: Evelyn A. Hellicar.

This church replaced a temporary iron church, although in this case one built privately by a local landowner. In 1926 the then Rochester diocesan architect, Evelyn Hellicar, was commissioned to design a new permanent church. As often occurred, he designed for more than could then be afforded, but in this case the chancel was added as soon as 1935, to his designs, although the architect himself had died by that time. The church is built in a simple red-brick neo-Perpendicular with a bare interior reflecting the strong Evangelical tradition of the parish (the post-War daughter church is dedicated to Bishop Ridley). The building has a slightly

odd appearance in that there is no west door, as might be expected: the main door is to the south, because it was originally intended to run a new road over Danson Park, on to which the door would open. In fact the road was never built and as a result the church has a more sylvan setting than many. In 1944 the church was hit by a flying bomb and the roof was repaired by the vicar and his congregation themselves.

Reference: Pevsner, 2, p. 152.

St Martin, Barnehurst

Status: in use.
Location: Erith Road, corner of Rudland Road.
Nearest station: Barnehurst.
Constructed: 1936.
Architect: P.M. Andrews.

This is an archetypal 1930s basilican building on a main road in an archetypal 1930s suburban area. It has flat-roofed aisles on either side of the main basilica and a small campanile at the east end. The main entrance is at the west end, over which there is a large circular window, and on the porch is an effective bas-relief of St Martin, giving some focus to otherwise unrelieved

Margaret Tarrant, generally with plenty of rabbits and birds in the foreground.' In fact the interior is now pleasant, with brick arches and white walls.

References: none.

St Mary the Virgin, Welling

Status: in use as a hall.
Location: Wickham Street, west side, between Sandringham Drive and Peters Close, opposite Shoulder of Mutton Green.
Nearest station: Welling.
Constructed: 1934.
Architect: T.F. Ford.

As well as designing the new church of St Michael, East Wickham, T.F. Ford designed what was originally a daughter church of St Mary. That took the form of a simple hall/church which was replaced by a new basilica in 1954, also by Ford. The original building remains in use as a hall, and is behind the new church.

Reference: Richardson, p. 176.

red brick. Andrews even designed a children's corner, a feature which has never recovered from the gentle sarcasm poked at it by Peter Anson in *Fashions in Church Furnishings*, where he remarked 'Hangings of a rather sickly shade of blue were almost obligatory, likewise framed reproductions of water colours by Miss

St Michael, East Wickham

Status: in use.
Location: Upper Wickham Lane, corner Okehampton Crescent.
Nearest Station: Welling.
Constructed: 1933.
Architect: T.F. Ford.

This church, unlike much of Bexley, is in the Diocese of Southwark rather than that of Rochester. As at Greenford, there was a small mediaeval church in the suburb, and the new church was built next to it: here, the old church is now used by the Orthodox. Thomas Ford was asked to provide a large church at low cost, which he did, the whole costing just under £10,000. The architect designed a substantial basilica, with an apse at the east end, which is well back from the main road and separated from it by an area of green. The land falls away at the east, which enabled storage rooms to be incorporated at a lower level than the main church. On each side of the main church are aisles, parts of which have since been converted to ancillary accommodation, and all the windows are simple and round headed. The interior is cream plaster with arches between nave and aisles and a timber roof. The font and pulpit are stone and original. In the 1970s brasses and other objects were introduced from the old church, and the interior was reordered by removing the reredos, setting up an icon of Christ in Glory in its place, and pulling forwards the altar.

References: Pevsner, 2, p. 144; Richardson, p. 49.

BRENT

St Andrew, Kingsbury

Status: in use.
Location: Church Lane, corner of Village Mews.
Nearest station: Wembley Park.
Reconstructed: 1934.
Architect: W.A. Forsyth.

The removal of the Victorian church of St Andrew, Wells Street, to Kingsbury, where it was urgently needed to replace one of the typical small Middlesex churches of a previous era, was remarkable, not only as a

feat of engineering, but also because it showed a respect for the building and furnishings of the Victorians which was unusual in the 1930s. The transplanted church suits its present village green surroundings remarkably well. It was built in 1847 by S.W. Daukes & Hamilton and was furnished and glazed by many of the great ecclesiastical architects of the nineteenth century - Burges, Butterfield, Pearson, Pugin and Street among others - as well as having glass by Clayton & Bell. The Anglo-Catholic tradition of the original church has been maintained in its new location.

References: Pevsner, 3, p. 135; VCHM, 5, p. 85.

St Andrew, Sudbury

Status: in use.
Location: Harrow Road, north side, near junction with Church Gardens.

Nearest station: Sudbury & Harrow Road.
Constructed: 1925.
Architect: W. Charles Waymouth.

This is a rather more interesting church than it first appears. It was designed by Waymouth, the architect for the London Diocesan Home Mission, to replace a mission church in Arts & Crafts style and which is now used as the hall. It had originally been intended to build a permanent church designed by J.S. Alder, but this was delayed by the outset of the First World War and then by his death. After the War the rapid increase in population in the area meant that a new church was required urgently.

Waymouth designed a red-brick free Gothic church with a barn-like interior, no tower or spire, but a simple bellcote over the south porch. The north and south walls have a lower tier of six relatively small windows on each side, and then above an upper tier of six neo-Tudor dormer windows. The east and west ends have large windows derived from the Perpendicular style. Inside there are brick piers supporting the heavy wooden roof: the original plan to have wooden pillars was abandoned. The area where the church was built was subject to flooding and in 1955 it was found that the pillars were moving and so steel rods were inserted across the nave to strengthen the construction.

References: Pevsner, 3, p. 140; VCHM, 4, p. 259.

St Augustine, Wembley Park

Status: demolished and replaced by new church.
Former location: Wembley Hill Road, corner of Forty Avenue.
Constructed: 1926.
Architect: T.H. Lyon.

The former church of St Augustine, Wembley Park, provides one of the most unusual stories of any of its time. In 1912 the Rev. G.S. Day was appointed as first missioner of a London Diocesan Home Mission area and a wooden hall was erected in 1913. In 1924 he was appointed chaplain of the Empire Exhibition church of St George and he used that position as a platform from which to procure money for a new permanent church for Wembley Park, fundraising by selling models and postcards of the design. Some £6,000 was then raised by the Diocese from the sale of St Mary, Vincent Square, which was demolished in 1923.

Plans were prepared for a Byzantine-style building to the designs of T.H. Lyon (1870-1953), then the head of the School of Architecture at the University of Cambridge. Lyon successfully built or added to a number of buildings in Cambridge, including work for his old college, Corpus Christi, and the lady chapel in Little St Mary, but he appears only to have built two other complete churches apart from Wembley Park, namely St George, Goodwood, Adelaide, South Australia (1903) and St George, Chesterton, Cambridge (1938). The latter has been plagued by damp from the time it was built, but St Augustine was more fatally flawed.

(Photo above is of old furnishings in the replacement church).

The original design was on a grand scale and would have cost some £30,000 to build, a massive sum at the time. As it was, funds were sufficient only for the construction of the chancel, round apse, chapel, vestries and two of the four planned bays of the nave. The dominant feature of the church however was its enormous height, standing well above the parades of shops and semis around. There were round-headed windows on both sides of the nave, and a circular window in the temporary west wall. The church developed a very strong Anglo-Catholic tradition, and as late as 1949 a new marble altar with reredos was installed which led to muttering in high places about the use of the Roman rite. However, cracks had appeared in the walls after bombs fell in the vicinity in 1942, and by 1950 the situation was so serious that the parish were told to evacuate the building immediately. Investigation revealed subsidence was occurring as a result of the combination of poor design and fragile subsoil, and the decision was taken not to rebuild the church, which would have been inordinately expensive, but to demolish it and reuse certain materials. In 1953 a new hall was erected as a prelude to a new church, but in 1973 a further hall was built and the 1953 building became the permanent church: it was extended in 1979. Apart from the reuse of bricks, there are some furnishings by Lyon from the 1926 church, including a very large wall rood set and a pair of enormous standard candlesticks.

References: none.

———————————————

St Catherine, Neasden

Status: in use.
Location: Dudden Hill Lane, north side, at junction with Dollis Hill Lane.
Nearest station: Neasden.

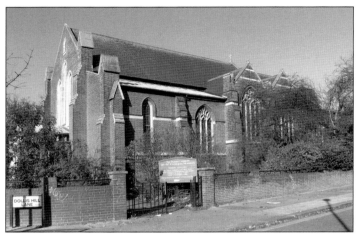

Constructed: 1916.
Architect: J.S. Alder.

This is an entirely conventional red-brick church in neo-Decorated style, one of the last designed by the prolific J.S. Alder. He originally planned for it a very considerable tower at the south-west corner and a large window for the west wall, but funds permitted the construction of neither. Three bays only of the nave were built together with the chancel, which was given a clear five-light window. The internal arches are of pale stone. In 1935 funds were sought to complete the church, but

this was not actually accomplished until 1954 when E.B. Glanfield added a simple west front with Early English lancets and a poorly detailed porch which juts out from it. The area is now somewhat run down and the church belongs in spirit more to the Edwardian than to the interwar years.

References: Pevsner, 3, p. 138; VCHM, 7, p. 239.

St Francis of Assisi, Gladstone Park

Status: in use.
Location: Fleetwood Road, south side, junction with Cullingworth Road.
Nearest station: Dollis Hill.
Constructed: 1933.
Architect: J. Harold Gibbons.

Not only is this church dedicated to St Francis, in common with many others built during this period, but its construction was also loosely based on the lower church at Assisi. Gibbons (1878-1958) was an ingenious architect who was not afraid to take up novel ideas. Here, he designed the white brick, low cruciform

church for a central altar placed beneath the crossing, a daring innovation at the time. In addition there was an altar in the east chapel behind it. The church has aisles and transepts on both sides and a small central bellcote providing a landmark among the contemporary semi-detached houses around. The Assisi theme is developed in the rounded concrete arches within and the round window on the west front. There is excellent glass by M.E. Aldrich Rope which was installed as the church was built, and a mural by James Bateman. The church is now run with St Andrew, Willesden Green: it has always had an Anglo-Catholic tradition, and is now a Forward in Faith parish.

References: Pevsner, 3, p. 127; VCHM, 7, p. 239.

St Michael, Tokyngton

Status: in use.
Location: St Michael's Avenue, junction with Babington Rise.
Nearest station: Stonebridge Park.
Constructed: 1932.
Architect: Cyril Farey.

The Diocese revived the name of a mediaeval chantry which had ceased to exist in the eighteenth century for a temporary hall which was opened in 1926. This self-conscious archaism stressed the continuity of the area with its past, but may not have attracted those who thought of Wembley as a new suburb. In 1932

the hall was replaced by a large, plain red-brick basilica by Cyril Farey, in a much more simple form than his later churches at Grange Park, North Greenford, and Teddington. Farey had in fact designed a spire but that, together with a chancel and lady chapel, could not be afforded when the church was first built, although substantial funds were made available for it from the sale of Christ Church, Endell Street, in the West End, together with much of the furniture from that source and choir stalls from St Paul's Cathedral. Farey's basilica has a large round west window and simple, square-headed windows in the nave, a whitewashed interior and round

headed arches. Initially there was a temporary apse for the sanctuary, but in January 1941 the church was bombed and the roof and windows destroyed. A new east end was added after the damage was repaired, and was consecrated in 1966: it is even plainer than Farey's design and presents a flat wall to the world, relieved only by a large cross. There is a concrete statue of St Michael over the north porch and a small bellcote: the bells came from St Thomas, Portman Square. The church is rendered more impressive than perhaps this description indicates by its position in an open grass area, enabling it to have considerable visual impact.

References: Pevsner, 3, p. 142; VCHM, 4, p. 259.

St Paul, Oxgate

Status: used as Hindu Temple.
Location: Dollis Hill Lane, opposite Mount Road.
Nearest station: Cricklewood.
Constructed: 1939.
Architect: N.F. Cachemaille-Day.

light the interior, and there is a very large east window with a statue of Jesus Light of the World in front of the central concrete strip. The window is one of the few designed by the architect himself, in modernistic style depicting angels. In contrast, there are carved teak choir stalls from a City church and some German glass from an unspecified demolished church. This building is deteriorating and needs attention if it is to be saved: it appears to have some use by Hindus.

References: Pevsner, 2, p. 127; VCHM, 7, p. 241.

This church had an extremely short life for the purpose for which it was intended. It was consecrated on 25 June 1939, replacing a temporary building on the same site, and was made redundant as early as 1980, a reflection perhaps of the changing ethnic make-up of the area in which it stands. The congregation migrated to St Catherine, Neasden.

The church stands up from the road with steps leading to it, but there is no tower or other feature drawing attention to it. Externally the concrete frame is faced with grey brick. Cachemaille-Day here employed, possibly for the first time, an almost flat vaulting using the exposed concrete construction to build the four-bay nave with aisles and one chapel. The liturgical west front (which actually faces south) has extraordinarily narrow slit-like windows on either side of a large concrete cross: without it, the building could easily be taken for a penal establishment. On either side are the box-like, flat-roofed aisles with small three light windows on each side. Cachemaille-Day used clerestory windows, which are not readily visible externally, to

CHURCHES NOT REQUIRING FULL ENTRIES

All Saints, Queensbury

A hall/church was built in 1938 in Waltham Drive. It still stands, but is now a hall only as in 1954 a large new church was built to the designs of R.B. Craze.

The Annunciation, Wembley

This is sometimes known as The Annunciation, South Kenton, and is in Windermere Drive. A tin mission church was built in 1938 which is now the hall: a modern church was built behind it in 1960.

The Ascension, Preston

A hall/church was built in The Avenue by Mitchell & Bridgwater in 1937 to replace a marquee. A permanent church was planned but delayed by the war and not constructed until 1957 (a late work by J.H. Gibbons). The original building adjoins it and is now used solely as a hall.

St Cuthbert, North Wembley

A wooden hall/church was built in 1938 in Carlton Avenue West, but was bombed in 1940. A new hall, followed by a church, was built after the war.

St Raphael, Neasden

In 1926 a temporary church was moved to Garden Way from a location on the Great Central Estate, where it had been erected in 1910. It was used for many years but has now been demolished and not replaced.

BROMLEY

Christ Church, Orpington

Status: in use.
Location: Charterhouse Road, opposite Malvern Road.
Nearest station: Chelsfield.
Constructed: 1940.
Architects: George True & Dunn.

This church combines a neo-Byzantine basilica-like structure with high walls with neo-Gothic windows. This uneasy mixture is not improved by the pink wash which has been applied to the west wall, nor even more so by the hideous modern porch extension in front of that wall which features a cross picked out by light bulbs. The tradition is strongly Evangelical and the lack of interior furnishings reflects that.

References: none.

St Andrew, Bromley

Status: in use.
Location: Burnt Ash Lane, east side, south of Milk Street.

Nearest station: Sundridge Park.
Constructed: 1929.
Architect: Sir Charles Nicholson.

This church replaced a series of mission rooms. It falls far below Nicholson's usual high standards of finish and in particular the bricks used are of poor quality. A small church with a rectangular shape incorporating a chapel, it has a campanile on the west front. The windows in the walls are tall and narrow and within brick arches. There is a foundation stone recording that masonic ceremonies were used at its laying. There are a considerable number of stained glass windows by the architect's brother, A.K. Nicholson, and the interior is better than the exterior. The tradition is of moderate Anglo-Catholicism.

Reference: Pevsner, 2, p.165.

St Augustine, Beckenham

Status: converted for residential use.
Location: Churchfields Road, corner Sultan Street.
Nearest station: Clock House.
Constructed: 1933.
Architect: G. Sworder Powell.

This former daughter church is now closed and has been converted into flats, which are known as St Augustine's Court. The roofline and aisles can still be seen externally, as can the clerestory windows, which were domestic-looking even before the conversion.

References: none.

St Francis of Assisi, Petts Wood

Status: in use.
Location: Willett Way corner with Greencourt Road.
Nearest station: Petts Wood.
Constructed: 1934.
Architect: G.T. Mullins.

This church fits well into the garden suburb atmosphere of Petts Wood and indeed a preserved area of the woodland from which the area took its name surrounds it. Local architect Geoffrey Mullins designed a competent but undemonstrative church in reddish brick, without tower, and is commemorated by a tablet in it. A lady chapel protrudes to the north. The windows are neo-Early English and the interior is of unpainted brick, with an English altar as originally installed and a new nave altar in front of it. The church is kept open and has a daily mass - an example of how Anglo-Catholicism did in some cases migrate successfully to new suburbs and flourish.

References: Pevsner, 2, p. 191; NCI, p. 82.

St Francis of Assisi, West Wickham

Status: in use.
Location: Ravenswood Avenue, west side, north of High Street junction.
Nearest station: West Wickham.

Constructed: 1935.
Architects: Newberry & Fowler.

This church is another careful but somewhat uninspiring production of Newberry & Fowler. It replaced a chapel dedicated to St Augustine. St Francis was a frequently-used dedication between the wars. The church as built was of cream coloured sand-lime bricks, and a square tower was built with the nave, chancel and south aisle. Newberry & Fowler had provided for a north aisle

to be added in due course, and this was done as late as 1973. The style was neo-Perpendicular and there is a particularly fine west window with extensive tracery. Inside there are five arches in the nave, and a rood screen which was salvaged from a bombed church in Folkestone. This church was itself bombed, and the east window blown out. It was replaced by a temporary window until a replacement showing St Francis was installed in 1980. Services now alternate with those at St Mary (q.v.).

Reference: Pevsner, 2, p. 196.

St James, Elmers End

Status: in use.
Location: St James Avenue, west side, near junction with Croydon Road.
Extended: 1934.
Architect: G. Sworder Powell.

This church qualifies for inclusion here because in 1934 the original, rather heavy Victorian building was

doubled in size by the erection next to it of a substantial extension by G. Sworder Powell. The effect from the exterior is of two churches side by side. The extension is a high-quality neo-Perpendicular in a much lighter brick than the strident red of the Victorian church, with fine wide windows and equally wide arches on the arcades within. It has an Anglo-Catholic tradition.

References: Pevsner, 2, p. 159.

St John the Baptist, Beckenham

Status: in use.
Location: Eden Park Avenue, east side, south of Merlin Grove.
Nearest station: Eden Park.
Constructed: 1936.
Architect: W. Pite Son & Fairweather.

This church is sometimes known as St John the Baptist, Eden Park. It is a substantial basilica with small campanile in red brick in an affluent-looking suburb. The oddest feature is perhaps the main entrance on the west wall, which has echoes of contemporary cinemas. There

are no side aisles and it was designed so that the whole congregation could have an uninterrupted view of the chancel: indeed a continuous rail was erected right across the chancel and the side chapel: unfortunately the interior has since been reordered and the altar is on the south side, completely disturbing the original conception. The roof is of decorated timber panels. The side windows of the nave are relatively narrow, but there are large rose windows at each end. The interior walls are plastered, with stone facings. *The Builder* said at the time that it was 'a departure from traditional char-acteristics', but it has worn well.

Reference: NCI, p. 28.

St Mary, Green Street Green

Status: in use.
Location: World's End Lane, opposite Dowlerville Road.
Nearest station: Chelsfield.
Constructed: 1937.
Architects: Newberry & Fowler.

This church, sometimes known as St Mary, Chelsfield, is on the very edge of the built-up area of Greater London, with open fields beyond it. It is another stock production from Newberry & Fowler, in a pale brick neo-Gothic, relatively low but with a small bell-tower. The church as built had only a nave without aisles and a sanctuary with transepts on each side, and was subsequently extended by the construction of a chancel. There is a rose window at the west end and neo-Perpendicular windows on each side. The interior is uncluttered but unmemorable.

References: none.

St Mary, West Wickham

Status: in use as church hall.
Location: The Avenue, north side, east of junction with The Drive.
Nearest Station: West Wickham.

Constructed: 1934.
Architect: Martin Travers.

In 1934 Travers constructed for his patron Father Shaw Page of West Wickham, for whom he carried out other work, a church/hall in rather undistinguished style. This was used for worship until the building in 1954 of the present church of St Mary of Nazareth by C.W. Fowler (successor to the Newberry practice), which was joined to it. It is again now used as a hall, save on special occasions when it can be used as an extension to the church, and a false ceiling has been added and a wooden floor laid. However, two plaques from the reredos in the hall are on the wall in the lady chapel above the new church, and there are Travers candlesticks in both that chapel and the main church.

References: none.

CHURCH NOT REQUIRING A FULL ENTRY

St Edward the Confessor, Mottingham

This is a church hall in St Keverne Road which was used as a church from its construction in 1937 until the building of a permanent church next door in 1957. It remains in use on what is now a dismal estate.

CAMDEN

St Benet & All Saints, Kentish Town

Status: in use.
Location: Lupton Street, east side, corner of Ospringe Road.
Nearest station: Tufnell Park.
Reconstructed: 1928.
Architect: C.G. Hare.

A nave for St Benet & All Saints was built by Joseph Peacock in 1885. In 1908 C.G. Hare, the successor to the practice of the great Victorian master Bodley, built a chancel on to it. The church qualifies for entry in this book because in 1928 Hare replaced Peacock's nave by a fine nave of his own, largely funded by a legacy from Jeanette Elizabeth Crossthwaite, who is commemorated on the refoundation stone. The church has a fine position on the crest of a hill, and Hare provided a tall, imposing nave with large windows and gables above. Its position means that even without a tower the church dominates the street scene. There is a strong Anglo-Catholic tradition and the furnishings match, including a rood by Hare himself.

Reference: Pevsner, 4, p. 345.

CROYDON

St Francis of Assisi, Coulsdon

Status: in use by Coptic Church.
Location: Rickman Hill, opposite Westleigh Avenue.
Nearest station: Woodmansterne.
Constructed: 1928.
Architects: Mathews & Ridley.

The first church in the Diocese of Southwark dedicated to St Francis of Assisi was this church/hall, built in 1928 as a mission of St Andrew, Coulsdon: other such dedications followed. It is more sophisticated than many such: it has aisles and a clerestory and stands high above the hill on which it was built. Although there were plans for a permanent church, none was ever built, and the congregation fell away. In 1989 it was sold to the Copts, who continue to use it.

Reference: Richardson, p. 34.

red-brick building in a simple Gothic style with lancets and very large transepts for the remarkably low price of £5,580. The economy in price was obviously not reflected in the materials, as it has lasted well and is extremely well kept. Inside, there are sharp arches and a single lancet on the east wall. A painting was executed for the chapel by the so-called fairy painter, Cicely Barker.

References: Pevsner, 2, p. 208; NCI, p. 15.

St George, Waddon

Status: in use.
Location: Barrow Road, east side, north of junction with Thorneloe Gardens.
Nearest station: Waddon.
Constructed: 1932.
Architect: W. Curtis Green.

This is the only church built in London during this period by the distinguished architectural draughtsman W. Curtis Green (1875-1960). It is hidden in a maze of narrow streets, many now one way. Green designed a

St James, Riddlesdown

Status: in use.
Location: St James Road, west side, opposite The Pines.
Nearest station: Riddlesdown.
Constructed: 1915.
Architects: Greenaway & Newberry.

This is an extremely fine church which benefits from its elevated position looking over the suburb. A mission church was built in the area in 1903 and enlarged in 1909. It became clear that that was insufficient, and Greenaway & Newberry were asked to design a permanent church. The original design had a substantial tower rising from the south transept and a five bay-nave. It was decided however to build the three western bays of the nave first, and this was duly done: aisles, and a baptistery at the west end was also constructed. At that time the church was known as St James, Coulsdon, but in due course it became a separate parish and took on its present name. In 1930 Newberry & Fowler substantially enlarged the church by adding a fourth bay to the nave and also a chancel with a chapel on the north side and vestries on the south. The tower was never built, although a turret was produced at the corner of

the vestries in which a bell could be hung. Newberry himself was the architect most concerned with the building on both occasions, and the result was a traditional building, well executed in neo-Decorated Gothic with appropriately styled windows. The stonework is particularly noteworthy.

The church was much enhanced thereafter by fine stained glass and other work by Martin Travers and his sometime assistant Douglas Purnell. Travers designed early, brightly coloured windows in the south aisle at about the time of the building and in 1916 a window to Mary Bloxam, which was in the north aisle but has now been moved to the south following vandalism. Following the enlargement he carried out further work, consisting of a window for the new chapel showing Mary with her Child in front of an emerald green Tree of Life. On the left is depicted Southwark Cathedral, on the right St James' church itself. In 1937 a baroque/Deco aumbry and ornate sanctuary lamp bracket were provided in this chapel, which were designed by Travers but actually carved by Purnell. Travers designed further work for this church after the Second World War, most of which was not completed, but after his untimely death in 1948 his pupil Lawrence Lee completed his design for a new east window of fine quality, and Purnell then designed a Second World War memorial on the south wall with St George and the Dragon depicted in Travers style. This is a very fine but little-appreciated building.

Reference: Richardson, p. 120.

St John the Divine, Selsdon

Status: in use.
Location: Upper Selsdon Road, west side, near junction with Addington Road.
Nearest station: Sanderstead.
Constructed: 1935.
Architects: Newberry & Fowler.

The *Buildings of England* volume says of this church, in typically sniffy fashion: 'A satisfying design, once one accepts lancet windows, etc. as fitting for 1935.' In fact

it is a standard Newberry & Fowler production: neo-Gothic, red brick, very competently executed. There is a tower at the north-east corner which barely rises above the roofline, and narrow aisles with seven light windows. A tall three light window is behind the high altar. The interior is light and pleasant. The chancel and lady chapel are not original: they were destroyed by bombing in the War but rebuilt to the same design.

Reference: Pevsner, 2, p. 228.

St Jude, Thornton Heath

Status: in use.
Location: Thornton Road, corner Gonville Road.
Nearest station: Thornton Heath.
Constructed: 1926.
Architects: W. Pite Son & Fairweather.

This is a very large church in a main road position. Although it has a prominent tower, the architects' original design, created before the First World War, for a spire on top of the tower was never realised and it

simply has a conical roof. Their revised designs prepared for the actual building in 1927 were more modest. The church is of red brick, neo-Decorated, and very well kept. It has a four-bay nave and chancel with continuous roof over both. There are aisles on both sides. The design was therefore extremely conservative, and even featured a raised chancel floor with further steps up to the high altar itself. Martin Travers designed the window of the Good Shepherd.

References: none.

St Mary, Sanderstead

Status: in use.
Location: Purley Oaks Road, south side, corner of Beech Avenue.
Nearest station: Purley Oaks.
Constructed: 1926.
Architects: Greenaway & Newberry.

This is an early example of a standard neo-Gothic design which was used with variations by Greenaway & Newberry in other places, such as East Sheen and

Nearest station: East Croydon.
Constructed: 1931.
Architect: C.G. Hare.

This was almost certainly the last church designed by Cecil Greenwood Hare, the successor to the Bodley tradition and practice. He died in 1932 before the ini-

Furzedown. As originally built, only three of the intended four bays of the nave were constructed: the fourth and the west end were left for later completion. The church is of red brick, with aisles each side of the nave and plain lancet windows. The roof covers both nave and aisles. The west end was not completed until 1970-1 when Stephen Dykes Bower finished the work in a style compatible with the existing work: he was one of the few architects by that date who would have been ready to do that, or even capable of it. The interior has high arches between nave and aisles and makes good use of space, as is to be expected from the architects concerned. Despite describing itself as having a Liberal Catholic tradition, it is now the subject of a Local Ecumenical Project with the URC.

References: Pevsner, 2, p. 228; Richardson, p. 140.

St Mildred, Addiscombe

Status: in use.
Location: Sefton Road, west side, corner of Bingham Road.

tial work had been finished, and in any event extension work was started almost immediately and carried out in 1933-4. The parish history, *The Story of St. Mildred's*

Addiscombe by C.W. Budden and R.R. Hutchinson (J.N. Clayton, 1937) recounts that Hare was an extremely agreeable man, but not very reliable when it came to the calculation of expenditure. Any parish employing Hare can only have wanted a very traditional design and they were given it, although the church is extremely large – a true cathedral of the suburbs. It is of lightish red brick, with squat central tower and neo-Decorated windows, including three-light examples on either side of the tower and at the west end and a rose window at the east end. The interior is more Classical in tone, with, it has been aptly said, some cinema overtones in the furnishings, especially the reredos.

Reference: Pevsner, 2, p. 210.

St Oswald, Norbury

Status: in use.
Location: St Oswald's Road, corner of Green Lane .
Nearest station: Norbury.
Constructed: 1934.
Architect: Caröe & Passmore.

St Oswald, Norbury, is a competently executed basilica built for the remarkably low price of some £7,500. Norbury was at that time still in the separated portion of the Diocese of Canterbury, which had no general appeal for funds such as that in Southwark. Caröe & Passmore used Byzantine precedents to create a simple structure of red brick with rounded windows, an apse at the east end and a gallery at the west end. A small tower with conical roof stands at the north-west corner, which interestingly does not feature on the original perspective drawings used to raise money for the project. The Byzantine theme is continued inside, with round-headed arches separating the nave from the aisles.

Reference: NCI, p. 110.

CHURCHES NOT REQUIRING FULL ENTRIES

St George, Shirley
This is a church hall in The Glade, which was built in 1937. It resembles a large holiday camp chalet.

It was intended that a new church should be built from the proceeds of All Hallows, Lombard Street, but that money was used elsewhere (see All Hallows, Twickenham). A new church was erected here in 1952 in an odd style which beggars description.

St Swithun, Purley
This is a church hall in Grovelands Road, designed by S. Jupp, which was used as a church from its construction in 1929 pending the building of a permanent church. Cachemaille-Day designed a new church next door and work began in 1939, but stopped because of the war. After the war, the part-built walls were demolished and a new church erected to designs by D.E. Nye. See Richardson, p. 110.

EALING

All Hallows, North Greenford

Status: in use.
Location: Horsenden Lane North, corner of Elton Avenue.
Nearest station: Sudbury Hill.
Constructed: 1941.
Architect: Cyril Farey.

This was the last permanent church built in London before the continuing hostilities of World War II brought church-building work to a halt, followed by post-war stringency which prevented a recommencement for some ten years or more. It was a development of a mission from Holy Cross, Greenford, which had provided a standard Forty Five Churches Fund hall in 1931. The plans for a replacement church were commenced in 1939, but then halted for a time. However the Diocese decided to press ahead with this and a number of other

schemes, and the foundation stone was laid in 1940. The dedication was derived from All Hallows, Lombard Street, the sale of which provided much needed funds for this building as for the similarly dedicated church at Twickenham. Cyril Farey designed here a squat central tower, as he had done in other places, but with the altar underneath the crossing and a lady chapel behind it. Because of the demand for materials, the required licences for the timber roof and the furnishing of the lady chapel were refused, so flat concrete roofs were provided over the nave and the lady chapel, and the latter was left unfinished. The high altar was designed with an arch behind it through which the lady chapel could be seen, but initially that was blocked off. The building is constructed of light bricks, and whitewashed inside. The nave and lady chapel windows are simple oblongs, but a circular window was fitted at the east end of the apse which was later filled by a fine Christ in Glory by Wilhelmina Geddes. The font came from the bombed All Hallows, Poplar, and furniture came from St Catherine Coleman, Hammersmith, after it too was damaged. In 1949 All Hallows became a parish and later that year the lady chapel was completed. By the 1970s the flat roof was leaking badly and was replaced by a pitched roof in accordance with the architect's original idea. This church is exceptionally well cared for and is attractively situated on the edge of a large area of open land.

References: Pevsner, 3, p. 181; VCHM, 3, p. 218.

Holy Cross, Greenford

Status: in use.
Location: Ferrymead Gardens, north side, near junction with Oldfield Lane South.
Nearest station: Greenford.
Constructed: 1939.
Architect: A.E. Richardson.

Professor Albert Richardson is usually considered as an arch-conservative in architectural terms. However, this unusual building shows him to have been capable of original design as well. By the mid-1930s Greenford was one of the most populous parishes in the Diocese of London. The old Holy Cross church is tiny and although a substantial number of missions had been commenced around, there was still a need for a new central church. Richardson originally intended to incorporate the old church into his new construction, but it was later decided to build separately but on an adjoining site, so the old church was refurbished and has continued to be used for some services.

Richardson built a large church, mainly of timber, along lines he had developed earlier at St Christopher, Luton. The walls are low and the building is visually dominated by the roof, which sweeps down to the walls on all four sides, broken by a row of clerestory windows. The main entrance is at the west end and stands forward, a large oriel window rising from it, and above that a small copper covered spire which emerges through the roof.

Internally, there is a forest of timber in all directions.

This church has been much-, perhaps over-, praised. One of its problems is that it was designed as a powerhouse for the spread of Anglo-Catholicism in the western suburbs. The high altar was provided with a canopy and dossal and was elevated on steps above the congregation in the then conventional way: there was a lady chapel behind and above it, in a rather more unconventional manner. The interior has now been radically altered: the high altar and the lady chapel are disused and a new central altar installed which adversely affects the ambience of the whole building. The pulpit is disused and in a corner.

References: Pevsner, 3, p. 181; VCHM, 3, p. 217.

St Barnabas, North Ealing

Status: in use.
Location: Pitshanger Lane, junction Denison Road.
Nearest station: Hanger Lane.
Constructed: 1916.
Architect: Ernest Shearman.

Shearman's third London church, but his first within the scope of this book, shows many of his characteristics. Like the later St Francis, Isleworth, it is at odds with its surroundings: in this case it is out of scale with the low cottage homes of the Brentham Estate among which it stands. It was also a less than happy commission for Shearman, who was dismissed before the work was completed after a series of misunderstandings which included the builders hoisting 15,000 bricks on to the roof because they were not told that a projected pair of towers on the west front had been abandoned: there was also a problem over the quality of the timber. Shearman was replaced by local architect, E.A. Tyler of Ealing.

The church is of dark, purplish brick with contrasting bands of stone facing. The characteristic Gothic windows, especially powerful around the apse behind the high altar, are complemented by a virtuoso rose window in the south chapel with tracery of astonishing complexity, and another on the west wall. A north chapel was never built. The lack of completed towers does not detract from the visual effect of the high pitched roof. The interior is full of vistas with clever Shearman touches everywhere. Although he had had his difficulties here, he was called back in 1926 to produce a statue of St Barnabas in memory of the first vicar, the Rev. Walter Mitchell. In 1936 a room designed by Shearman was added above the sacristy on the north side of the chancel. The church also has an impressive mural in the sanctuary by James Clark, which was painted in 1917, and a number of windows by Clayton & Bell. There is a strong Anglo-Catholic tradition, as usual with Shearman's churches.

References: Pevsner, 3, p. 165; VCHM, 7, p. 152.

St Barnabas, Northolt Park

Status: in use.
Location: The Fairway, north side, at junction with Raglan Way.
Nearest station: Northolt Park.
Constructed: 1939.
Architect: J. Harold Gibbons.

This church has some similarities with the architect's contemporary St Mary, Kenton. It was commenced before the war, but not finally finished until 1954. Gibbons built, as at Kenton, in a personal adaptation of

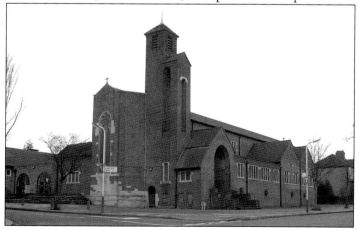

the Gothic style and in a similar pale brick. The nave is tall and thin, with a large window at the west end, and flat-roofed aisles on either side. The visual effect of the south aisle, which faces a wide but quiet dual carriageway in a quintessentially leafy suburb, is somewhat adversely affected by a disproportionately large porch and short gabled transepts, and also by the simple squared windows, which contrast with the more elaborate western light. Behind the porch rises a very slender tower with pointed roof and a slightly lower bellcote in front with a look of Scandinavia about it. The interior is mainly concrete, some painted, with clever use of a variety of roof forms.

References: Pevsner, 3, p 186; VCHM, 4, p. 121.

St Edward the Confessor, Perivale Park

Status: in use: now known as Holy Trinity local ecumenical partnership.
Location: Medway Drive, corner Suez Avenue.
Nearest station: South Greenford.
Constructed: 1936.
Architect: N.F. Cachemaille-Day.

The hall/church of St Edward, Perivale Park, was one of the missions established by Holy Cross, Greenford. Its interest lies in the fact that it was designed by Cachemaille-Day, who used his usual ingenuity to provide, for the very modest sum of £2,780, a much more commodious building than was usual for such a project. As originally constructed, the main part of the hall was a simple brick-built rectangle with a stage at one end. At the other, three round-headed arches with plain round columns (made from cast-iron drainpipes) led through to a small chancel and sanctuary, which could be shut off when required. To the side of the sanctuary was a two-storey section with vestries on the first floor, joined to the hall by a quarter-circular kitchen area: above it was a small bell-tower. The money for this construction was given anonymously. In 1998 the nearby URC church was demolished and an extension constructed to St Edward, which is now a so-called local ecumenical partnership. The exterior has been rendered but Cachemaille-Day's ingenuity remains beneath all the changes.

Reference: Pevsner, 2, p. 655.

St Gabriel, North Acton

Status: in use.
Location: Noel Road, near junction with Balfour Road.
Nearest station: Acton Main Line.
Constructed: 1929.
Architect: Ernest Shearman.

Shearman's penultimate London church has some considerable similarities to his earlier St Barnabas, North Ealing, and even more to his bombed St Matthew, Wimbledon, which was built before the First World

War. Although a large building, it has remained unfinished and the west end was constructed of cheap bricks as a temporary wall and has remained in place: economy was also effected in cutting down the number of windows originally designed. The red-brick church has no tower but, as at St Barnabas, rises high above the neighbourhood and has clerestory windows set up in the walls and narrow lancet windows around the east end apse. There is a very elaborate south transept rose window with characteristic Shearman tracery. The interior is of red brick with Gothic arches. The tradi-

tion is one of Anglo-Catholicism, again consistent with Shearman's churches, although in recent years a nave altar has been installed which detracts from the original design.

References: Pevsner, 3, p. 155; VCHM, 7, p. 38.

St Peter, Acton Green

Status: in use.
Location: Southfield Road, junction with St Alban's Avenue.
Nearest station: South Acton.
Constructed: 1915.
Architect: W.A. Pite.

St Peter, Acton Green, is a substantial basilica with a wide nave and narrow processional aisles, and an apse at the east end. The contemporary records indicate that it was intended to erect a 75-foot campanile, but that was never done. It was however provided with early ferro-concrete pillars inside and a west gallery containing the organ, which was a relatively unusual feature by the date it was built. The exterior is of yellow brick, now well weathered, with red-brick facing and some stone

around the west door. Chairs instead of pews were used here before they were fashionable, and the high altar was provided with a tall reredos, and elevated on steps, making it readily visible throughout the church. The reredos has since been removed. A screen was erected from the Quebec Chapel, which was demolished just before this church was built and replaced by the new church of The Annunciation, Marble Arch. St Peter's was in the forefront of the Anglo-Catholic Movement under Father T.C. Calvert, who was one of the 'Twenty One' who defied Bishop Winnington-Ingram's lightly administered ban on Benediction in the late 1920s, and then after 1938 under Father W.G. de Lara Wilson, who was a great supporter of the Walsingham devotion and in 1942 commissioned Martin Travers to produce a backing of Our Lady, which he claimed to have designed himself.

References: Pevsner, 3, p. 156; VCHM, 7, p. 38.

St Saviour, Acton

Status: in use.
Location: Old Oak Lane, corner Armstrong Road.
Nearest station: Acton Central.

Constructed: 1924.
Architect: Sir Edward Maufe.

Maufe's two churches for the deaf, this and St Bede, Clapham, are very similar. In both locations he built over existing social rooms, and here in particular, although the church is proportionately very tall, it is also quite short. It also shares a number of features with his later church of St Thomas, Hanwell. The church took its dedication from the earlier church for the deaf of St Saviour, Oxford Street. Maufe built in light red

brick with well-executed Gothic windows, a four-light one on the west wall, three lancets on each side of the nave and one each side of the chancel. There is glass by Travers in the side chapel. The floor is slightly raked, as at Clapham, and there are two pulpits, also as at Clapham.

References: Pevsner, 3, p. 156; VCHM, 7, p. 38.

St Thomas the Apostle, Acton Vale

Status: demolished.
Former location: Bromyard Avenue, in central island.
Constructed: 1915.
Architect: A.C. Blomfield.

In 1915 A.C. Blomfield (1863-1935) built a somewhat undistinguished Gothic church in a prominent central island site on Bromyard Avenue, off the Uxbridge Road, around which it had been intended to build a garden city. The dedication to St Thomas came about as a result of funds being provided from the sale of St Thomas, Charterhouse, from which also passed the churchwarden's staves and some other items. It replaced an iron mission church of St Barnabas. Blomfield built only two-and-a-half bays of the nave, transepts, a chancel with polygonal apse and a lady chapel with similar but smaller and separate apse. In 1937-9 the church was substantially extended westward by C.H. Biddulph-Pinchard, who was presumably related to the two brothers of the same name who were Anglo-Catholic priests. He added three bays to the nave. Although the roof-line was continued, he did not add to the aisles and his new windows were influenced more by the Perpendicular than by the existing Decorated. The west end was quite plain with a statue of St Thomas above. At one time this church was home to some exotic devotions and had a chapel of the Seven Sorrows of Our Lady. A small parish room was added to the north of the nave as late as 1972-3, but by the end of that decade the church was being considered for redundancy, and was later demolished: it has been replaced by flats named Canterbury Court.

References: Pevsner, 3, p. 157; VCHM, 7, p. 38.

St Thomas the Apostle, Hanwell

Status: in use.
Location: Boston Road, opposite Chepstow Road.
Nearest station: Boston Manor.
Constructed: 1934.
Architect: Sir Edward Maufe.

There is a strong argument that this is the finest church of its era in London. It has also benefited from being very well kept and from the recent (1995 onwards) restorations, which, instead of destroying what was designed, have aimed to restore the original decora-

tions. Further, it is frequently open, an example followed by all too few other churches. Maufe had won the competition for the new cathedral at Guildford in 1932, but in the meantime he designed this church, which was finished before work began in Guildford in 1936. He used it as a testing ground for some of his ideas for the cathedral, particularly the reinforced concrete vault with acoustic plaster and the silver grey Tondu bricks from South Wales. He built a seven-bay nave with passage aisles, and a one-bay chancel with one-bay sanctuary. The nave is tall but at the south-east corner the architect built a square tower with copper cap which stands above, but does not take away from, the main building. The windows are lancets, derived from but not slavish copies of, Early English. Some windows in the tower have tracery in the pattern of spears to signify the patron saint. Maufe also designed a lady chapel and (typical of the age) a children's corner, although this one was much more tastefully furnished than those at which Peter Anson memorably poked fun, and has survived. The church was also fortunate in that furnishings were supplied by a number of well-known artists of the day, and, in addition, some items, especially the reredos (by Cecil Hare in the Bodley tradition) and the organ came here from the demolished St Thomas, Portman Square, the sale of which released funds for the building here. The most prominent external feature is a large crucifix with attendant rood figures by Eric Gill, which cleverly stands against the circular east window and uses its tracery for support.

Internally, the dominant colour is white, against which the furnishings stand out. Vernon Hill carved the stone font and also the dove above the doors. The lady chapel has an English altar, again retained, designed by Maufe himself, a Madonna and Child by Hill and the ceiling was decorated by Kathleen Roberts. The children's chapel reredos has a nativity scene in which the church itself can be seen in the background and was the work of Elizabeth Starling. There is glass by Moira Forsyth in the same chapel and behind the font. Maufe designed silver-plated light fittings for the church with the arms of the apostles.

References: Pevsner, 3, p. 184; VCHM, 3, p. 233; NCI, p. 36.

The Ascension, Hanger Hill

Status: in use.
Location: Hanger Lane corner of Beaufort Road.
Nearest station: Hanger Lane.
Constructed: 1938.
Architects: Seely & Paget.

This extremely well-kept church in spotless grounds not far off the North Circular Road is a curious mixture of styles, as is often the case with any building by Seely & Paget. It is of pale brick over concrete, although there is much stone facing on the tower. The plain west front has an empty niche above the door and is topped by a pediment of Classical derivation. The nave has

simple square-headed windows both in the walls and in dormer windows above: the central tower, by contrast,

has much taller round-headed windows and there are similar, smaller, lights in the upper storey of the double semi-circles which form the apse at the east end. To add to the visual effects, there are balustrades on all four sides of the tower. This is certainly an unusual church externally, although internally more conventional.

References: Pevsner, 3, p. 165; VCHM, 7, p. 152.

CHURCHES NOT REQUIRING FULL ENTRIES

Holy Redeemer, Greenford

The mission church of the Holy Redeemer was built in Windmill Lane in 1930 and was the first to be built by the Forty-Five Churches Fund. It closely resembled the still-existing hall at All Saints, Hillingdon. It was demolished, as was another contemporary mission in Allenby Road, Southall, following the construction of the new church of Christ the Redeemer, Southall, in 1964.

St Christopher, Hanwell

This temporary building in Bordars Road was built in 1937 and demolished in 2003/4 when a new church was built in partnership with a development by the YMCA.

St John, West Ealing

This church qualifies for this book since, although built in 1876, it was the subject of substantial rebuilding by F. Hall-Jones in 1923 following a fire in 1920: a tower remains but the spire was demolished as part of the reconstruction.

St Joseph, Northolt

A temporary building in Watery Lane was opened in about 1942 but abandoned within two years or so. In due course a new church was opened on another site.

St Mary, West Twyford

This odd corner of the capital saw a hall opened in 1937 for the small chapel adjacent. In 1958 Cachemaille-Day built on to the chapel a substantial new church, but that is now closed and access is prohibited as it is dangerous. The congregation now uses the hall.

St Nicholas, Perivale

A hall of standard design was opened in 1934 to replace the small old parish church. In 1963 a new church was opened in front of it, but the hall remains.

ENFIELD

St Peter, Grange Park

Status: in use.
Location: Vera Avenue, corner of Onslow Gardens.
Nearest station: Grange Park.
Constructed: 1940.
Architect: Cyril Farey.

This church, in a very pleasant and prosperous suburb, had been planned in 1939 but the scheme was deferred on the outbreak of war. The Diocese of London, however, decided at the beginning of 1940 to go ahead with the construction of six new churches, and this building was begun that year and consecrated in 1941. Farey designed a substantial building, in light brick with a squat crossing tower and very long chancel. The windows are rectangular save on the west wall and the apse behind the altar, where there are roundels. The well-kept interior is white-plastered with rounded arches. The most interesting aspect of the building was the use

made of material and furnishings from other London churches. The roofing timber came from St Mary, Islington, St Paul, Bethnal Green, St Paul, Edgware Road, and St Stephen, Bow. The pews and pulpit were from St Etheldreda, Fulham, the choir stalls from St Stephen, Poplar, and the bell from St John, Drury Lane. The font and altar rails were originally in St Katherine Coleman in the City, and then went to the new St Catherine Coleman, Hammersmith, which was bombed. This is an impressive church, particularly bearing in mind the circumstances in which it was constructed. There is later stained glass by M. Aldrich Rope.

References: Pevsner, 4, p. 456; VCHM, 5, p. 249.

SS. Peter & Paul, Enfield Lock

Status: demolished and replaced.
Former location: Ordnance Road.
Constructed: 1928.
Architect: not known.

This church was built to replace the chapel in the Royal Small Arms factory, which was closed in 1921. It was a chapel of ease to St James, Enfield Highway, and was dedicated in May 1928. It was a simple brick building with a small bell-tower over the west wall and domestic-looking windows protruding from the roof. Judging from the birettas worn at the dedication, the tradition was always Anglo-Catholic. On 27 June 1944 the church was destroyed by a V1 bomb in an incident which saw three people killed and eleven seriously injured. A new church was built to replace it on a nearby site and was consecrated in 1969.

Reference: VCHM, 5, p. 249.

St Thomas, Oakwood

Status: in use.
Location: Prince George Avenue, at northern end of Sheringham Avenue.
Nearest station: Oakwood.
Constructed: 1939.
Architects: Milner & Craze.

An iron chapel of St Thomas was erected in Winchmore Hill Road in the early years of the twentieth century, and it was intended that a permanent church on the same site would replace it. However, as the suburb of Oakwood grew with the coming of the tube, it was decided to sell the site to the local authority, and the proceeds, together with money from the sale of St Thomas, Portman Square and St James' vicarage, Shoreditch, were used for the construction of a new church in Oakwood itself. R.B. Craze had to cut back on his original design because of the war and omitted the west end with apse. He built a simple brick building with flat panelled roof and apsidal chancel. The interior is whitewashed. In 1965 William Mulvey completed the building with a simple west end and a distinctive copper spire. The latter blew down in 1974 and was rebuilt.

References: Pevsner, 5, p. 456; VCHM, 5, p. 187.

GREENWICH

All Saints, New Eltham

Status: in use.
Location: Bercta Road, east side, corner Bishop's Close.
Nearest station: New Eltham.
Extended: 1930.
Architect: T.F. Ford.

All Saints, New Eltham, was built in 1898 and then consisted of a nave with a temporary timber-framed apse as its chancel. After the First World War the population in the area increased rapidly and it was decided to enlarge the church. The original architect, Peter Dollar, was still in practice but he was passed over in favour of T.F. Ford, who added a neo-Perpendicular chancel and made other improvements, almost doubling the capacity. An English altar was installed. In 1939 Ford returned to install a new west end, including a large Perpendicular window. The church was damaged in the Second World War but restored.

References: Pevsner, 2, p. 279; Richardson, p. 100.

St Barnabas, Eltham

Status: in use.
Location: Rochester Way, north side, near Well Hall Roundabout.
Nearest station: Eltham.
Reconstructed: 1933.
Architect: T.F. Ford.

This is undoubtedly one of the oddest churches in London. It began life as the Royal Dockyard Chapel in Woolwich and was designed by Sir George Gilbert Scott. In 1916 a hut church had been provided for the Well Hall area, but by the early 1930s the population had increased dramatically and further provision was

1946 an internal hut was erected within the walls of the church to enable services to continue. An extraordinary transformation occurred in 1956-7 using the same architect as before: while the walls and roof were restored approximately to their previous design, the interior was completely remodelled in a neo-Classical style with a barrel-vaulted ceiling and an apse mural by Hans Feibusch. The result is an interior which does not match the exterior and an exterior which does not match the area.

References: Pevsner, 2, p. 280; Richardson, p. 53.

St Saviour, Eltham

urgently required. It is interesting that, in an era when Victorian churches were not highly regarded, it was decided to take down the Dockyard Chapel and reuse it for this area: the cost involved was £13,000, for which a substantial new church could have been built. Ford rebuilt the church on Rochester Way, omitting the galleries and in other ways slightly modifying it, but retaining its character. In 1944 it was burnt out by bombs, leaving only the external walls. The congregation migrated temporarily to the church hall, but in

Status: in use.
Location: Middle Park Avenue, south side, at corner of Churchbury Road.
Nearest station: Mottingham.

Constructed: 1932.
Architects: Welch, Cachemaille-Day & Lander.

Probably the best-known London church of the era is this one, by Cachemaille-Day placed strategically in the middle of what is now a fairly run-down estate. Unfortunately, the exterior has been marred by graffiti and litter is strewn in the doorways: there is no notice board to indicate signs of life. This church, although famous, is entirely atypical of the new churches being built at the time, and also, paradoxically, although it has a novel exterior and construction, the underlying plan is extremely traditional. The total cost of £11,000 odd was also no more than would have been the case with a more conventional building at the time. It was also built in advance of most of the houses on what was then a completely new estate. Cachemaille-Day used reinforced concrete for the building, but cased the walls in dark brick. At the ritual west end he designed a tower which is large but squat, barely rising above the nave. As elsewhere, he added a protruding stair turret to it. The nave windows are extremely narrow and very tall, giving a fortress like effect from the outside.

The interior features the clever use of brick, especially shown in the pulpit, which seems to grow out from the wall: even the altar rails, reading desk and clergy stalls are in brick. The dominant feature of the interior is however a nine-feet-high concrete sculpture of Christ holding the world in his hand, by Donald Hastings, which is the centre of a reredos also made of concrete. A huge cross hangs from the ceiling in lieu of a rood. There is a lady chapel, also with a reredos of concrete, and a west gallery with organ and provision for the choir. Undoubtedly St Saviour is an important church: whether it is more or less successful than Cachemaille-Day's more traditional designs is perhaps a matter for the observer.

References: Pevsner, 2, p. 281; NCI, p. 114; Richardson, p. 60.

CHURCH NOT REQUIRING A FULL ENTRY

St Saviour's Mission Hall, Eltham

This was a forerunner of St Saviour, Middle Park Avenue, and was a timber hall erected in Mayerne Road in 1929. It then became the parish hall of the new church, but in 1957 was reopened for a short time as St George's Mission Church. In 1961 it was demolished. See Richardson, p. 58.

HACKNEY

CHURCH NOT REQUIRING A FULL ENTRY

St John of Beverley, Stoke Newington

A church for the deaf was built on Green Lanes in 1920. It was destroyed by fire in 1960.

HAMMERSMITH & FULHAM

St Catherine Coleman, Hammersmith

Status: demolished after bombing but rebuilt as a new church.
Former location: Westway, north side, west of Primula Street.
Constructed: 1922.
Architect: R. Atkinson.

St Catherine Coleman was a substantial church designed by Robert Atkinson, better known for his secular architecture. It replaced the mission church of St Michael, Du Cane Road, which was dedicated in 1915 and closed in 1923. Its replacement took its name and many of its furnishings from the former City church of St Katherine (sic) Coleman, Fenchurch Street, which closed in 1921. The first vicar of the new church was Father L.S. Beale, who had been at St Michael's since 1918 and remained with St Catherine until 1955. He established the tone of Anglo-Catholicism which influenced the furnishings of the new church from the

very beginning. Atkinson built a simple basilica type building of brick, with a round window at the west end, six round-headed windows high along the north and south sides, and a windowless six-sided apse at the east end. The high altar was draped with a tasselled canopy in the then fashionable style and there was a mural above. A number of items were placed there from the former City church, including the altar rails. The church was heavily bombed in the war and had to be demolished, although in the immediate aftermath the parishioners held a service in the ruins. The congregation migrated temporarily to the mission church of St Andrew, Primula Street, until a new church designed by J.R. Atkinson, the son of the original architect, was built on the foundations of the old but omitting the apse: it was, of course, in a completely different style. The church was renamed St Katherine, reverting to the original spelling but omitting the Coleman, and still retains the altar rails from the City church, which alone of all the furnishings from that source survived the war. Both churches are alternatively described as being in East Acton.

References: none.

CHURCH NOT REQUIRING A FULL ENTRY

St Andrew, East Acton
Nothing has come to light about this mission church in Primula Street save that it was opened in 1930 and is no longer in existence.

HARINGEY

St John the Baptist, Tottenham

Status: in use.
Location: Great Cambridge Road, between Acacia Avenue and Laburnum Avenue.
Nearest station: White Hart Lane.
Constructed: 1940.
Architects: Seely & Paget.

This church replaced the mission church of St Hilda, which was built on the corner of Great Cambridge Road and White Hart Lane in 1926. It was largely paid for by the sale of St John the Baptist, Marlborough Street, which was demolished in 1937. It is a curious building which uses red brick and concrete but manages to look neither traditional nor daring. The nave is tall and rectangular, with six large oblong windows set high up on each side with copper cladding around them, which gives the entire building a strange contrast now that it is green with age. Over the main entrance on the west wall there is a very large statue of the saint to whom the church is dedicated, under a copper

half-dome supported by four columns, with a Classical portico behind the dome. The interior is more successful, with good use of space from the concrete arches and extensive whitewashing on the walls. There is also a gallery.

References: Pevsner, 4, p. 572; VCHM, 5, p.355.

St Matthew, Muswell Hill

Status: demolished.
Former location: Creighton Avenue, north side, corner of Coppetts Road.
Constructed: 1939.
Architects: Caröe & Passmore.

This church had an extraordinarily short life. In 1926 a mission church was erected in Coppetts Road, and in 1933-4 came a larger hall/church. The permanent

composition in red brick with stylised Gothic-derived windows and an entrance porch on the west wall. The interior was refined with good fittings. It is an indictment of the Church of England that it was unable to attract a sufficient congregation to such a fine church in a very pleasant middle-class neighbourhood.

Reference: VCHM, 6, p. 175.

church was built in 1939 and closed in 1978: it was demolished in 1981. Caröe drew a perspective for the new church as early as 1931, but it appears that when it came to be built his partner Herbert Passmore carried out much of the work. Caröe had designed a substantial tower with spire above on the west front, but that was never built. Passmore substituted a tower with its own gabled roof on the south side. The church was a careful

CHURCHES NOT REQUIRING FULL ENTRIES

Good Shepherd, Wood Green

In 1916 an iron church was moved from Neasden and erected in Berwick Road at the corner of Stirling Road. It was replaced after the Second World War by a small brick-built building which is now used by an Eritrean Church.

St Gabriel, Bounds Green

After the demolition in 1983 of the church of 1905, the hall on the corner of Bounds Green and Durnford Roads was used as the church until it too was demolished in 2004. The hall had been built in 1936 and was used as an air raid shelter during the War.

HARROW

St Alban, North Harrow

Status: in use.
Location: The Ridgeway, between Norwood Drive and Church Drive.
Nearest station: North Harrow.
Constructed: 1936.
Architect: A.W. Kenyon.

This very large church, its size if anything accentuated by the open space in which it stands, was much

praised at the time of its construction and has been lauded since. Some may take the view however that, unlike some more conventional productions of the time, it now appears somewhat dated. Kenyon won the commission after a competition. He moved away completely from Gothic precedents, while at the same time retaining an entirely customary lay out. The building is of brown brick with a shallow-pitched copper roof and a substantial flat-roofed tower to the south-east with a look of contemporary Scandinavia or Holland. The east end is completely devoid of decoration or breaks and now seems to resemble a warehouse wall: at the west is a porch with double round-headed doors and one small window toward its top. The aisles have tall narrow windows, also with round heads, but a slightly stepped effect: the clerestory above has small six-sided lights. The interior is white with tunnel vaulting and ambones, an idea original at the time, but, as the *Buildings of England* volume notes, cheapened since by its use in coffee bars.

References: Pevsner, 3, p. 260; VCHM, 4, p. 260; FMC, p. 86.

St Anselm, Belmont

Status: in use.
Location: Uppingham Avenue, corner of Clifton Avenue.
Nearest station: Canons Park.

Constructed: 1938.
Architect: N.F. Cachemaille-Day.

Cachemaille-Day himself had worshipped at St Anselm, Davies Street, Mayfair, a church built in the neo-Byzantine style as recently as 1891. It was therefore fitting that he should design the large new church of St

Anselm, Belmont, which took its name from the West End church and also inherited many fittings from it on its demolition: two paintings had in fact already passed to that parish from the Hanover Chapel in Regent Street.

Cachemaille-Day was here much more conventional than in many other places: he built a tall, towerless brick basilica with a striking, uninterrupted semi-circular apse around the sanctuary. He reused the large west window and the smaller nave windows, all with fine stone tracery, which had been in the Davies Street building, but the small round-headed clerestory windows are his. The internal stone columns are also from Davies Street. The church was not completed until 1941, and was one of the last to be finished in London before wartime austerity put paid to ecclesiastical building for some years, and contemporary accounts make it clear that the building was only permitted to proceed because of the economies resulting from the reuse of materials.

Reference: Pevsner, 2, p. 299.

St John the Baptist, Greenhill

Status: in use.
Location: Sheepcote Road, corner Station Road.
Nearest station: Harrow on the Hill.
Extended: 1938.
Architect: Martin Travers.

This church was built by J.S. Alder in 1904 with a Gothic nave and clerestories. It finds its way into this book because, two extensions between the wars. In 1925 Alder & Turrill lengthened the nave towards the east to enlarge the church, and then in 1938 Martin Travers added a new chancel and chapel, rather surprisingly at a lower height than the nave. The intended tower was not completed because of the onset of hostilities and remains as a base alone. The difference in height between chancel and nave was filled above the chancel arch by a tympanum of Christ in Glory, flanked by Our Lady and St John, all on a background of stars. Travers also installed a light screen (since unfortunately removed) in the nave, an English altar (since altered) and other woodwork, tablets, and glass. The church is well kept and despite the double extension looks appropriate for its prominent town centre site.

References: Pevsner, 3, p. 260; VCHM, 4, p. 258.

St Mary the Virgin, Kenton

Status: in use.
Location: Kenton Road, corner St Leonard's Avenue.
Nearest station: Kenton.
Constructed: 1936.
Architect: J. Harold Gibbons.
St Mary, Kenton, was the successor to a half-timbered temporary church dedicated to St Leonard, commemorated in the street name of the adjoining road. The dedication changed when the permanent church was built because it received substantial funds from the sale

of the site of St Mary, Charing Cross Road, the foundation stone of which is in the new building. St Mary, Kenton is among the most distinguished churches of its era in London, and certainly is one of the most lavishly furnished, a reflection of the efforts of the first parish priest, Father F.R. Johnson.

The church stands well back from the road, with the clergy house and ancillary rooms at a right angle to it running down to the highway. There is thus a garden and paved area in front of the church itself which enables it to be appreciated from a distance. Gibbons built in a personal Gothic, very different from his earlier St Francis, Gladstone Park, in light brick with stone facings. The main visual feature of the exterior is a tower on the south side, from which runs an external cloister leading to the ancillary block. The tower has a particularly fine two-light window in its base. There are lancet windows in the nave and a further pair of very tall lights above the west door with a large statue of Our Lady and the Holy Child between them: the statue is by Herbert Palliser, Professor of Sculpture at the Royal Academy, who also carved the font and the stations of the cross. Gibbons' ingenuity is best demonstrated here by the lady chapel, which he placed, unconventionally, behind the high altar and at an elevation, with the vestry beneath.

The interior is largely original, with unpainted concrete walls but decorated wooden roofs. The church had from the beginning a strong Anglo-Catholic aura, as had the Charing Cross Road parish, and this is reflected in the rood and other contemporary interior fittings. In addition, however, Father Johnson procured a small mediaeval angel from the font of St Giles, Cripplegate, some stained glass from All Saints, York, and, for the baptistery, Italian glass.

References: Pevsner, 3, p. 281; VCHM, 4, p. 259; FMC, p. 49.

St Paul, South Harrow

Status: in use.
Location: Corbins Lane, corner of Reverend Close.
Nearest station: South Harrow.
Constructed: 1937.
Architect: N.F. Cachemaille-Day.

This is not one of Cachemaille-Day's more successful designs, although he had a difficult site with which to deal, long and narrow in shape. The *Buildings of England* volume described it as 'one of his more daring modernist buildings' but in fact it now looks neither daring nor modern. The squat tower faces the road with five tall slit windows on all three external sides and a turret staircase surmounted by a concrete cross. Behind, the body of the church is warehouse-like, with similar slit windows at intervals along the sides. In front of and to the side of the tower Cachemaille-Day placed a low extension for vestries and a chapel, to which has now been added a particularly unfortunate porch. The chancel is directly beneath the tower. Because of the restrictions imposed by the site, the architect designed only one aisle, on the north side, which is separated from the nave by a conventional arcade. The contemporary reports in *The Builder* indicate that, contrary to first impressions on looking at the building, much of it is constructed of brick with the roof being of timber. The flat roofs are concrete, and the exterior is rendered with lime and sand and coloured cream: this has discoloured over the years to an unpleasant greyish hue. The church is strongly Evangelical.

References: Pevsner, 3, p. 262; VCHM, 4, p. 259.

CHURCH NOT REQUIRING A FULL ENTRY

St Michael & All Angels, Harrow Weald

In 1935 a long, low brick hall with rounded windows was erected, which was used both for the church and as the chapel of Wykeham Hall, founded by New College, Oxford. In 1958 T. F. Ford designed a permanent church which was built on to it at right angles.

HAVERING

All Saints, Squirrels Heath

Status: bombed and rebuilt on a different site.
Former location: Squirrels Heath Road, corner of
Upper Brentwood Road.
Reconstructed: 1933.
Architect: J.J. Crowe.

The then hamlet of Squirrels Heath was provided with a
chapel of ease to Romford parish church in 1884 when
a small building was erected. The area developed and in
about 1914 it was enlarged by the addition of aisles on
each side. In 1927 a hall was built on an adjoining site,
designed by J.J. Crowe, who generously waived his fees.
In 1933 the same architect substantially reconstructed
the chapel by adding to it a chancel. The total effect
may not have been entirely aesthetically pleasing as
it is recorded that the temporary organ chamber and
heating apparatus on the north side resembled a factory rather than a church and it was necessary to plant
a shrubbery at that point to conceal it. The projected
new nave had not been built when, in 1941, the building was completely destroyed by a bomb. A post-war
church replaced it on a different site.

Reference: VCHE, 7, p. 86.

Architect: Newberry & Fowler.

Newberry & Fowler could not by any stretch of the
imagination be described as progressive architects, but
this church looks for all the world, even to the informed

Good Shepherd, Collier Row

Status: in use.
Location: Collier Row Lane, corner of Redriff Road.
Nearest station: Romford.
Constructed: 1934.

observer, that it was built 50 years before its actual construction. They even provided a tower at the north-east corner which provides a landmark among the suburban development. Dame Violet Wills, the benefactor of St Alban, Becontree, was again generous in her support here. The brick is pale and cool, the east window has stained glass while the wider east window floods the church with light through its clear glass. As always with Newberry & Fowler, the detail is good, especially the font supported by stone angels and the reredos, which is also of stone. This is a church of which architectural critics despair, but on the other hand has the invaluable asset of looking like a religious building in the eye of the casual passer by.

References: Pevsner, 5, p. 163; VCHE, 7, p. 86.

Holy Cross, Hornchurch

Status: in use.
Location: Hornchurch Road, corner of Park Lane.
Nearest station: Romford.
Constructed: 1933.
Architects: W. Pite, Son & Fairweather.

This church, of which the recent *Buildings of England* volume is unfairly disparaging, benefits from an excellent site, nearer Romford than Hornchurch, on a main road, and surrounded by well-kept grass which enables it to be appreciated at a distance. It replaced a hut which had previously been a chapel on an army camp. The large building is unaltered externally and was constructed for the remarkably low sum of £7,345. It is of red brick, cruciform in shape with a small turret at the crossing with a needle like spire. Although the side windows are narrow, there is a large round west window: above the altar are three square headed lancets. The interior is neo-Romanesque and is perhaps a disappointment, white washed and somewhat plain and not enhanced by a glutinous window commemorating a boy scout. However the arches along the nave are well executed and the church as a whole is underrated.

References: Pevsner, 5, p. 176; VCHE, 7, p.49; NCI, p. 124.

St Agnes, Romford

Status: in use.
Location: Jutsums Lane, opposite Bridport Avenue.
Nearest station: Romford.
Constructed: 1928.
Architect: Not known.

This little-known building is a remarkable survival. A mission church of the Anglo-Catholic parish church of St Andrew, Romford, it provides mass twice a week and at other times the simple blue and white hall is used for various community activities: perhaps it has a lesson for those seeking to maintain expensive and crumbling mediaeval buildings.

Reference: VCHE, 7, p. 86.

St George, Hornchurch

Status: in use.
Location: Kenilworth Gardens, corner of Connaught Road.

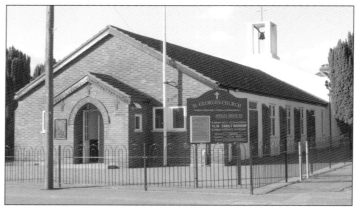

Nearest station: Hornchurch.
Constructed: 1931.
Architect: Not known.

This church was built as a chapel of ease to St Andrew, Hornchurch. The south end (liturgically west) looks for all the world like any of the other hall/churches built at the time, but the north (liturgically east), added later, has an apse of white concrete with a small bellcote and slit windows with undistinguished painted glass.

Reference: VCHE, 7, p. 49.

St John the Divine, Romford

Status: in use.
Location: Mawney Road, south of junction with Pretoria Road.
Nearest station: Romford.
Constructed: 1927.
Architect: W.D. Caröe.

This is a complicated church building, built over a number of years. A temporary iron church was erected on another site as early as 1897, and later extended. In 1926 the present site was purchased and W.D. Caröe commissioned to design the permanent church. He produced plans for a substantial basilican church based on Byzantine and Classical precedents, but at that stage all that could be afforded was the sanctuary, to which was then added a temporary building. Caröe's work is typically carefully detailed, with barrel vaulting featuring decorative plasterwork. The next stage of the building, in 1932, was under the supervision of Caröe's partner Herbert Passmore, who reduced the scale of the project considerably. He completed the choir, nave, side aisles and transepts and designed the striking dome over the crossing with light allowed to enter through windows high above. In 1948 a war memorial chapel was added and in 1968 a choir vestry. It became clear that completion to anything like the original size, which would have involved adding another three bays to the five added by Passmore, was unlikely, so in 1980 the temporary weatherboarded west wall was taken down and a brick replacement with entrance designed by Laurence King & Partners was erected. A clergy vestry was added over the choir vestry in 1985. Despite the number of additions made, the strength of Caröe's original design shines through and the completed church is successful as well as interesting. There is more information in Jennifer Freeman: *W.D. Caröe: His Architectural Achievement* (Manchester University Press, 1990), p. 82 ff.

References: Pevsner, 5, p. 192; VCHE, 7, p. 86.

St Michael & All Angels, Gidea Park

Status: in use.
Location: Main Road, north side, west of Links Avenue junction.
Nearest station: Gidea Park.
Constructed: 1938.
Architect: J.J. Crowe.

Gidea Park is Romford's own garden suburb, but the church of St Michael was not erected in the sub-

urb itself as originally planned. A mission hall from All Saints, Squirrels Heath, was erected in 1928 and replaced in 1933 by a better version. The permanent church followed in 1938. It is set back from the main road but with land around. Crowe designed a substantial red-brick church with a continuous roof over the nave, chancel and aisles and a tower on the south side which loses much of its visual impact by its very distance from the passing traffic. The tower has a copper roof over louvred walls, an attempt to identify with Essex churches of the past. The main building has relatively small neo-Jacobean windows which fail to emulate Nicholson's mastery of that idiom, although the interior is spacious and furnished impeccably to middle Anglican use, including a wooden Bishop's chair. It must also be said that the cost of the church was the very low sum of £6,500.

References: Pevsner, 5, p. 192; VCHE, 7, p. 86; FMC, p. 68.

St Peter, Harold Wood

Status: in use.
Location: Gubbins Lane, east side, north of Squirrels Heath Road.
Nearest station: Harold Wood.
Constructed: 1939.
Architect: J.J. Crowe.

Harold Hill is a prosperous suburb which was given an iron church as early as 1871, but had to wait until 1939 for a permanent building, after which it became a separate parish. In the meantime, the Rev. Bernard Hartley, who was in charge from 1913 and later the first vicar, had established a strong Evangelical tradition, which has continued. Crowe's building is based on traditional Gothic designs, including a castellated tower, and with lancet windows. The tower is topped with a green copper flèche. Substantial donations towards the building were made by the Matthews brothers, who were local millers. The visual effect of the building has been adversely affected by a crass low extension at the west end in debased Tudor, erected in 1963. The inte-rior is white, and the floor has been tiered and heavily carpeted in recent years in accordance with modern Protestant practice. The fittings are predictably plain.

References: Pevsner, 5, p. 167; VCHE, 7, p. 49.

CHURCHES NOT REQUIRING FULL ENTRIES

St George, Harold Hill

A temporary church was built on Straight Road in 1939, but was replaced by a new church in Chippenham Road in 1953, and no longer exists.

St Nicholas, Elm Park

A temporary church was built on St Nicholas Avenue in 1936 but replaced by a new building by J.J. Crowe in 1956 which looks at first and even second glance as if it were built in the interwar period.

HILLINGDON

All Saints, Hillingdon

Status: in use.
Location: Long Lane, corner of Ryefield Avenue.
Nearest station: Hillingdon.
Constructed: 1932.
Architect: Sir Charles Nicholson.

This church replaced a standard mission hall which has remained in use as the parish rooms, complete with original decorated brickwork on the façade. The church itself is of red brick, built by Nicholson with his usual care and having windows derived from the Perpendicular style. There is a small tower topped with

a copper pyramid on the south-west corner, barely rising above the pitch of the roof. The most unusual feature is the west front, looking on to the road, which has a curiously lop-sided appearance caused by the nave and the north aisle both finishing at that point but at different heights. At the east end of the same aisle is a

transept. The arches within are round headed, in contrast to the windows, and there is Kempe glass from the chapel of a preparatory school which closed as this church opened.

References: Pevsner, 3, p. 334; VCHM, 4, p. 91; NCI, p. 54.

St Anselm, Hayes

Status: in use.
Location: Station Road, corner of St Anselm's Road.
Nearest station: Hayes & Harlington.
Constructed: 1926.
Architect: H.C. Corlette.

Major Hubert Corlette (1869-1956), the Australian-born former partner of Sir Charles Nicholson, designed

this neo-Gothic church in the now dismal town centre area of Hayes, rendered the more unpleasant by a traffic management scheme which cuts off the streets to through traffic. The church is of yellow brick, now somewhat faded with age, edged with red brick. There is no tower, but a small bellcote and aisles on both sides of the nave with flat roofs. Internally, the architect provided stone Gothic arches between nave and aisle and there are sound three-light windows at each end of the nave, the west end facing on to the town centre. Decoration of the ceilings was by Macdonald Gill. The church has always had an Anglo-Catholic tradition,

and from 1944 to 1975 the parish priest was Father A.T. Phyall, a leading member of many pro-Roman organisations.

References: Pevsner, 3, p. 327; VCHM, 4, p. 36; NCI, p. 91.

St Jerome, Dawley

Status: in use.
Location: Dawley Road, corner of Judge Heath Lane.
Nearest station: Hayes & Harlington.
Constructed: 1933.
Architect: J. Harold Gibbons.

This large suburban church was provided not only with a substantial tower but also with a porte cochère beneath it large enough to drive a car through. The tower, at the west end, is now joined to a parish hall which was not part of the original construction. Gibbons built here in red brick, now looking somewhat the worse for wear because moss and lichen have disfigured large areas. There is a steeply-pitched roof which continues over the aisles, an apse at the east end,

and transepts. The windows are neo-Romanesque and, as with all Gibbons' churches, there are clever touches, such as the stepped effect on the tower, which repay close study. The interior has whitewashed arches and a great sense of space.

References: Pevsner, 3, p. 323; VCHM, 3, p. 272; NCI, p. 34.

St Lawrence, Eastcote

Status: in use.
Location: Bridle Road, south side, near junction with Field End Road.
Nearest station: Eastcote.
Reconstructed: 1932.
Architect: Sir Charles Nicholson.

Eastcote was originally part of Ruislip parish and had no ancient parish church. The area has remained more rural in feel than many in what was Middlesex, and Sir Charles Nicholson's design for St Lawrence suits it well. The land for the church was given by the Hawtrey fam-

ily of the now-demolished Eastcote House. Nicholson built - in red brick as usual - a church with aisles on both sides of the nave but here each was provided with its own steeply-pitched roof. He also built a tower at the south-east corner with a high gable at its top. The windows are round headed, although the west window ingeniously combines five round-headed lights within a Tudor-influenced outline. Inside, there is some use of 'beauty by inclusion' with Roman columns, round

arches, and a painted wooden screen. The east window is a memorial to the Rev. R.F. Godwin, missioner and then first priest of Eastcote, who stayed in the parish until 1956.

References: Pevsner, 3, p. 313; VCHM, 4, p. 144; NCI, p. 84.

St Paul, Ruislip

Status: in use.
Location: Tiverton Road, corner of Thurlestone Road.
Nearest station: Ruislip Gardens.

Constructed: 1936.
Architect: N.F. Cachemaille-Day.

At St Paul, Ruislip, Cachemaille-Day built a more conventional church than many of his designs. The building is of red brick, originally a simple basilica shape with high walls, a steeply-pitched roof and an apse at the east end. A large, flat-roofed south aisle was added in 1952: to the north are ancillary buildings. The clerestory windows are simple oblongs with a domestic air, but there is a circular west window with fine glass. The interior piers are lozenge-shaped. The building was funded from the sale of St Paul, Bunhill Row and some furniture was provided from the demolished St

Jude, Grays Inn Road. The interior has brick piers and whitewashed walls.

References: Pevsner, 3, p. 347; VCHM, 4, p. 144.

CHURCHES NOT REQUIRING FULL ENTRIES

Christ Church, Harlington
A hall/church was erected here off Waltham Avenue in 1936. In 1965 a curious box-shaped church was added to it.

St Edmund, Northwood Hills

A hall/church was erected in Pinner Road in 1935. In 1968 a new church resembling an aircraft hanger in shape was built next to it but the hall remains in use.

St Edmund, Yeading

A hall/church was erected here in Yeading Lane in 1933. A modern church was built in 1961 and there is also a replacement hall.

St Mary, South Ruislip

A hall was erected in The Fairway in 1931. It no longer stands, and was replaced by a modern church in 1959 which is a rare outpost of Forward in Faith in the suburbs.

St Nicholas, Hayes

A hall was erected in Balmoral Drive in 1937. It was later replaced by a new church and hall on a different site.

HOUNSLOW

All Saints, Heston

Status: in use.
Location: Broad Walk, north side, east of Springwell Road.
Nearest station: Hounslow West.
Constructed: 1938.
Architects: Seely & Paget.

This church and hall had the distinction of being designed by Seely & Paget and are thus more comely than many, the grey brick used being much more

attractive than the standard red. It has remained as a dual-purpose building rather than being superceded by a permanent church. The building is low and the windows square-headed and domestic in character.

References: VCHM, 3, p. 126; FMC, p. 126.

St Francis of Assisi, Isleworth

Status: in use.
Location: Great West Road, opposite Syon Park Gardens.
Nearest station: Syon Lane.

Constructed: 1933.
Architect: Ernest Shearman.

The last of Shearman's personal statements of Gothic was built in a particularly inappropriate location, although one where it makes an immediate visible impact. Its inappropriateness arises from the fact that it stands near the modernist factories of the Great West Road, and in stark contrast to them. The church was the subject of a generous benefaction from the Rev. F.H. Harding, who is commemorated on the foundation stone, and is immensely tall, although towerless, with the apse containing the sanctuary facing the main road. The narrow lancet windows light the apse and nave, and there are two of Shearman's characteristic rose windows, one with particularly elaborate stone tracery. Some of the chancel furniture came from St Mary, Charing Cross Road, and there is a tall narrow canopy (matching the

structure of the church) by Travers, over the statue of Our Lady in the side chapel.

References: Pevsner, 3, p. 438; VCHM, 3, p. 129.

CHURCHES NOT REQUIRING FULL ENTRIES

Holy Angels, Cranford

A temporary corrugated-iron mission was erected in 1935 off Bath Road, and nearer the centre of the new population than the old church in the park of the great house. In 1940 it was provided with its own priest, but in 1941 it burned down and was replaced the following year by a converted Rodney hut. The parish priest of Cranford at this time was the former secretary of the Anglo-Catholic Congress, Father Maurice Child, and he commissioned Martin Travers to design a baroque altar for this unpromising situation. This church was itself burned down in about 1965 and a new building was constructed in 1970 with the same dedication but in a different location.

St Mary, Isleworth

An unusual, partly weatherboarded hall/church was erected in Worton Road at the corner of Bridge Road in 1931. It served as the parish church until the construction of a permanent building designed by H.R. Goodhart-Rendel in the 1950s.

St Stephen, Hounslow.

Cachemaille-Day added a brick tower in 1935 to this church in St Stephen's Road built by Ewan Christian in 1875.

KENSINGTON & CHELSEA

St Francis of Assisi, North Kensington

Status: in use after long period of disuse.
Location: Dalgarno Way, north side.
Nearest station: Ladbroke Grove.
Constructed: 1935.
Architect: not known.

St Francis of Assisi, North Kensington, was built in 1935 and dedicated in 1936. It was constructed as a mission church in the parish of St Michael & All Angels, Ladbroke Grove, to serve the new St Quintin Estate area which was the last undeveloped corner of Kensington. The church is a simple brick-built barn shape with corrugated roof, but the west end, the only part visible from the road, has more than an air of the Spanish Mission about it. The subscribers to the building fund included T.S. Eliot, churchwarden of the neighbouring St Stephen, South Kensington.

The church was provided with an altar with papier maché baldachino above it and in due course was fashioned with cheap shrines and the like as befitted a centre of Anglican Papalism. The church was so out of the way that it appears that a blind eye was turned to some of the teaching which emanated from it - certainly in about 1970 it sported pamphlets by the CTS and there was a large outside crucifix high on the west wall. The façade was then painted white. In due course the social changes in the area and a declining congregation led to closure and the building was declared dangerous. In 2000 it was transferred to the neighbouring parish of St Helen, St Quintin Avenue, and in 2004 it was reopened for occasional services to rather a different character from before, although its main use is now by a Pentecostal group.

References: none.

KINGSTON-ON-THAMES

Emmanuel, Tolworth

Status: in use.
Location: Grand Avenue, west side, south of junction with Moresby Avenue.
Nearest station: Tolworth.
Constructed: 1935.
Architect: not known.

This building now conceals the original construction of 1935, which was a small brick church/hall set back

from the road with the altar at the east end in the conventional way. In the 1950s (or possibly slighter later) a wooden extension was built at the west end which included a new chancel and vestries: the orientation was thus reversed. There is a very large wooden gable with a cross on it: the *Buildings of England* volume calls it 'very successful' but it is now badly worn and even more badly dated.

Reference: Pevsner, 2, p. 324.

St George, Tolworth

Status: in use.
Location: Hamilton Avenue, corner of St George's Gardens.
Nearest station: Tolworth.
Constructed: 1934.
Architect: T.F. Ford.

This is an example where no permanent church followed the original church/hall, but subsequently a new building was erected to extend the facilities available. In 1934 T.F. Ford provided a simple hall with a chancel projecting from the east end (nearer the road) with a hipped copper roof. The cost of about £5,500

St James, New Malden

Status: in use.
Location: Malden Road, corner Bodley Road.
Nearest station: New Malden.
Constructed: 1934.
Architects: Newberry & Fowler.

was about 60% of the cost of a standard church at the time. Further efforts continued to build a permanent church, but the cost seemed prohibitive and in 1957 a new hall was erected at right angles to the first on the south side, enabling the earlier building to be used only as a church. Unfortunately the new hall was a disaster: it leaked and eventually was pulled down. The site was sold for building and a third hall erected on the north side of the original. The combined building is known as St George's Church Centre. The original hall remains in use for worship, although the altar is now on the south side rather than in the chancel.

References: Pevsner, 2, p. 324; Richardson, p. 164.

The traveller on the Kingston by-pass can see a tall, commanding red-brick church with a tower as he approaches the Malden turn off. This is St James, New Malden, one of Newberry & Fowler's more imposing productions, and one of the few where the tower was built as planned. It replaced a mission church of 1904. In 1929 Merton College, Oxford, conveyed the land on which a permanent church could be built and Bishop Garbett, as usual with him, ensured that the patronage of the new living would be in the hands of the Bishop of Southwark. This was probably no more than an expression of his centralised thinking on administration, but it raised concerns among those who took a party line. Malden had a strongly Evangelical tradition, and in this case the fears of that group were fulfilled as

the new church developed worship on the other side of the spectrum.

Newberry & Fowler designed and built a very traditional Gothic building with Perpendicular windows. There is a large seven-light window at the west end, a five-light window in the north transept, and the aisles are also generously lit. The nave has highly-placed clerestory windows which continue right round the apse at the east end, and there is no main east window: this gives the apse an unfinished look externally. The tower is also of very traditional build and stands well above the body of the church. In 1944 the west end was badly damaged in an air raid and the church was closed until 1947, but repair and improvement continued for some years thereafter. In 1958 the sanctuary was decorated to the design of J.B.S. Comper, Sir Ninian's son.

This is a very fine church and because it was so old-fashioned when it was built, it does not appear to have aged as much as some of its time.

References: Pevsner, 2, p. 321; Richardson, p. 79.

St John the Divine, New Malden

Status: in use.
Location: Kingston Road, south side, west of junction with California Road.
Nearest station: New Malden.
Constructed: 1939.
Architects: Newberry & Fowler.

Newberry & Fowler built two churches in New Malden, at opposite ends of the suburb. St James is imposing, whereas St John, although also executed in red brick with Perpendicular detail, is much less so. It also strongly reflects the Evangelical tradition of much of the area. It is a simple aisleless construction, competently executed even as the war broke out (the foundation stone was laid by Lady Kinnaird on 24 June 1939). A sanctuary with Early English windows was added in 1958. Unfortunately, in 1995 a transept was added at the west end which is elevated above a new entrance on pillars. This makes use of space within at various levels, but destroys the symmetry of the original building. The interior is plain and there are pinkish chairs.

References: none.

LAMBETH

Holy Redeemer, Streatham Vale

Status: in use.
Location: Streatham Vale, corner of Churchmore Road.
Nearest station: Streatham Common.
Constructed: 1932.
Architects: Martin Travers & T.F.W. Grant.

There are those who think that Martin Travers only carried out work for the ultramontane wing of the Church of England. In fact, he would work for whoever wanted to employ him and his work here and at Emmanuel, Leyton, was for Evangelicals. This is even more marked in the case of this church, which was designed as a memorial to the Evangelical Clapham Sect. A church/hall was designed by Sir Charles Nicholson, and opened in 1928 but it was soon followed by the permanent church, which was consecrated on 5 March 1932. The design, showing the interior looking east, was exhibited

by Travers at the Royal Academy in 1933. The church cost the considerable sum for the time of £11,775: Bishop Garbett waived his usual requirement that the patronage be vested in the Diocese because he thought that more money could be raised from Low Church groups by allowing the living to be held by the Church Pastoral Aid Society.

Holy Redeemer was built of stock bricks with pre-cast stone tracery in a modified fifteenth-century style. The chancel is a continuation of the nave. The roof was steel, covered with copper, and is topped with a small classical cupola with solid sides. Travers introduced many typical touches to the church. The hanging lights have some Baroque feel and were cut from sheet copper. The sanctuary is a modification of his usual style, again showing some Baroque influence, but with the Ten Commandments on plaques on either side of the clear east window. The reredos was ogee-shaped, of pleated wood painted red and gold, with a plain cross on it.

There were no candlesticks on the altar. The internal wooden furniture, such as the pews, was all designed by Travers, save for the lectern which came from elsewhere. The church has no painted glass at all: Travers anticipated that the east window would in due course be filled with stained glass, but this has never occurred. The church has been little altered internally although the original light fittings and the reredos are no longer there: the text boards remain, as do many of the furnishings.

References: Pevsner, 2, p.389; NCI, p. 150; Richardson, p. 156.

St Anselm, Kennington

Status: in use.
Location: Kennington Lane, corner of Sancroft Street.
Nearest station: Kennington.
Constructed: 1932.
Architects: Adshead & Ramsey.

This church is anomalous: it is the nearest church to the centre of London built during the era of this book. In fact a new church was erected in an area which already had a surfeit partly because the scheme began before the First World War with a more grandiose design featuring a domed edifice, and partly because Adshead, a distinguished town planner, was involved, with his partner Ramsey, in a far more wide-ranging scheme to revive the Prince of Wales' Kennington estate. In fact what was erected is a substantial basilica, plain on the outside with yellowish bricks which have aged and round-headed windows set high in the walls. The west end has a round window over the entrance. The unrelieved brick is broken by stone detailing around the doors. Inside, there are arcades with round arches, a side chapel and a baldachino over the high altar which was installed when the church was built. There is now a nave altar in front of it, which as always in those circumstances looks incongruous. The detailing of the font and other features is fine and there is carving on the panels above the doors. The building remains a well-executed and well-preserved example of the interwar basilica style.

References: Pevsner, 2, p. 334; NCI, p. 18.

St Bede, Clapham

Status: in use as social club.
Location: Clapham Road, west side, north of Clapham North station.
Nearest station: Clapham North.
Constructed: 1924.
Architect: Sir Edward Maufe.

Maufe built two churches for the deaf in the 1920s, of which this was one. He built it over the existing institute, so that the church itself was elevated. His design was a simple church in the Gothic idiom with special facilities such as a slightly tilted floor and a separate pulpit for a sign language interpreter. On either side of the chancel were small extensions, one of them forming a chapel and the other a vestry. The detail is careful and ingenious, as might be expected from an architect of Maufe's ability. There are star hanging lights as at St Saviour, Acton. The church was bombed in the war and rebuilt, and for the last ten years has been used by Copts. It is shortly to be demolished – a significant loss.

References: Pevsner, 2, p. 334; NCI, p. 59.

St Saviour, Ruskin Park

Status: in use.
Location: Herne Hill Road, corner Finsen Road.
Nearest station: Loughborough Junction.
Constructed: 1915.
Architect: A. Beresford Pite.

This church qualifies for this book only, as it were, by the back door. The Victorian church of St Saviour was made redundant in 1980 and pulled down in 1982, shortly before it would have fallen down. In 1987 the former church hall, built by Pite in 1915, was refurbished for use as a church, but with other community functions as well. It looks like a school, which it sometimes is, and is topped by two tall chimneys and a slate covered cupola. There are three arches over the entrance. It is an interesting building, but not overtly ecclesiastical.

References: none.

LEWISHAM

Holy Trinity, Sydenham

Status: in use.
Location: Trinity Path, off Sydenham Park.
Nearest station: Forest Hill.
Constructed: 1925.
Architect: E.C. Christmas.

Holy Trinity, Sydenham, now uses the former parish hall, which has replaced a large Victorian church which was demolished in 1982. The hall is a relatively small, domestic-looking red-brick building hidden away up a path between the houses. The patrons are the Simeon Trustees and the worship correspondingly Protestant in tone.

References: none.

St Barnabas, Downham

Status: in use.
Location: Downham Way, north side, corner Cinderford Way.
Nearest station: Grove Park.
Constructed: 1928.
Architect: Sir Charles Nicholson.

The huge Downham estate was begun in 1924. The Diocese of Southwark was, rightly, anxious not to be tardy with the building of new churches for the area and decided to follow the familiar pattern of erecting a hall first on a site which was large enough to take a

permanent church as well as soon as funds permitted. As at the adjoining development at Bellingham (q.v.) Sir Charles Nicholson was chosen for the project. He designed both the hall (1926) and the church (1928). As with other such new developments, the funding came almost entirely from the Twenty-Five Churches Fund, as there was no pre-existing nucleus of local support

from which to move forward. The site was particularly impressive, as the church was built on a bend in the main road through the estate, and thus faces down one side, forming a readily recognisable focus to the area. Nicholson built a substantial church utilising Byzantine and Classical precedents of red brick, with no tower but a simple bellcote on the west front. There is a large circular window on the west front but the other windows are rounded and simple: it is a mark of social conditions in the early twenty-first century that some have now to be protected from vandals by boarding. The flat-roofed aisles are internally divided from the nave by substantial columns. The starkness of the largely white interior was partly relieved by the introduction of Anglo-Catholic furnishings, including the peculiar use of six candlesticks on an English altar with painted reredos. In 1981 internal reordering, including the provision of a nave altar, took place. This is a successful design by Nicholson, although with few flourishes.

References: Pevsner, 2, p. 413; Richardson. p. 36.

St Dunstan, Bellingham

Status: in use.
Location: Bellingham Green, east side, near junction with Swallands Road.
Nearest station: Bellingham.
Constructed: 1925.
Architect: Sir Charles Nicholson.

The first church built with assistance from the Twenty-Five Churches Fund was St Dunstan, which succeeded a hall built in 1922. Its site on the Green, planned as the centre of the new estate, was an advantage to the architect. Nicholson designed a very large church indeed, which would have held almost 800 people,

but, perhaps fortunately in the light of the subsequent decline in churchgoing, his scheme was never realised in full. He built three of the four bays of the planned nave, but not the chancel. A temporary east wall was erected which has now been in place for 80 years. The west wall, which faces on to the Green, has a large five-light window in Gothic idiom over a seven-bay arcade with rounded arches. Beneath the arcade is an impressive main entrance, with the brick surrounds deriv-

121

ing some inspiration from the Continent, as does the bell-tower on the north-west corner. The church has for many years had a tradition of Anglo-Catholicism, and in recent times this has been allied to Socialism, a combination once familiar, now almost lost within the Church of England.

References: Pevsner 2, p. 414; Richardson, p. 15.

St John the Baptist, Southend

Status: in use.
Location: Bromley Road, east side, between Whitefoot Lane and Oldstead Road.

Nearest station: Bellingham.
Constructed: 1928.
Architect: Sir Charles Nicholson.

One of the most impressive churches built between the wars is St John the Baptist, Southend, which Garbett planned as a central church for the newly developed area, with the other new churches for Bellingham and Downham dependent on it. He was attempting to reproduce the so-called Portsea system, in which he had been trained. The vicar whom he appointed to St John, the Rev. E.F. Edge Partington, had himself been trained in Portsea, and he proved himself an able administrator. Prior to the construction of the church, the only place of worship in the area was a former

proprietary chapel which still stands next to it, but its capacity was such that it was clear that new provision had to be made.

Nicholson began designing as early as 1919 and produced two impressive sets of plans for a church of almost cathedral-like proportions. His last plan was cut down by the omission of three of the five bays of the nave and of the majestic tower, but even so the building cost £26,000, about twice the cost of most other churches of the time. Unlike St Dunstan, Bellingham, the east end and chancel were built as planned and a temporary west wall was erected: the church was built far enough back from the main road to leave a space for the projected extension. The portion of the nave which was built had substantial aisles on each side, and also massive transepts. The whole was constructed in red brick in a neo-Perpendicular style, but the consequence of the west wall being left unfinished is that it is a much more impressive building from the side or the east than it is to those passing on the busy road. The seven-light window on the chancel wall is invisible to the casual observer.

The interior is lofty and impressive, although more traditional than many of Nicholson's designs: in effect he recreates a Gothic church, with little of the drawing on other sources sometimes seen in his work. In 1977 an unfortunate reordering took place, which involved closing off the chancel and the provision of a central altar on the crossing, a scheme which fits ill with the architect's designs for the church as a whole. There is stained glass by Karl Parsons, and E. Liddell Armitage, the author of a standard work on the subject.

References: Pevsner 2, p. 414; Richardson, p. 148.

St Luke, Downham

Status: in use.
Location: Northover, east side, corner Shroffold Road.
Nearest station: Grove Park.
Constructed: 1937.
Architect: Sir Charles Nicholson.

The last of the churches built for the Downham area was St Luke, which replaced a hall opened in 1930 to serve the northern part of the estate. It was a less ambitious design than St Barnabas, and much less prominent, both because of its back-street location and because the building was more modest in its elevation, although it has a small bell-tower. The windows are neo-Tudor and it was built in red brick with aisles. In 1941 it was damaged by a fire bomb and required substantial repairs after the war.

Reference: Richardson, p. 41.

MERTON

St George, Merton

Status: in use.
Location: Central Road, opposite Willows Avenue.
Nearest station: Morden South.
Constructed: 1932.
Architect: T.N. Ashford.

This inconspicuous, domestic-looking, building represents a failure in Bishop Garbett's vision for the Diocese of Southwark. He wanted to take part of the former parish of Morden into a new St Helier parish, but he was foiled by the strong opposition from that parish which feared a watering down of their strong Protestant form of worship. After a prospective donor

had fallen away, the plan to build a permanent daughter church to Morden parish church also disappeared, and a hall was built, designed by T.N. Ashford. Funds for a larger structure still did not appear, so in 1938 a wooden building was erected next to the hall and used for worship. In 1976 the roles of the two buildings were reversed: the hall was renovated and now forms the church and the wooden building was rebuilt to form a family centre, the two being linked by a new structure. The church is low, of red brick with a high-pitched roof and seven gables on each side. The interior is sparsely decorated, as may be expected, with a black and white timbered roof.

References: Pevsner, 2, p. 447; Richardson, p. 97.

St Olave, Mitcham

Status: in use.
Location: Church Walk, off Rowan Road.
Nearest station: Norbury.
Constructed: 1931.
Architect: A.C. Martin.

This church is very near Holy Redeemer, Streatham,

each being near the edge of their respective boroughs. It has a hidden location in a cul-de-sac in rather dismal surroundings. A new hall was built in 1927-8 and was rapidly followed by a permanent church, designed by Arthur Martin (1875-1963). The finance for the project came largely from the proceeds of the sale of the former St Olave, Tooley Street, Southwark, from which the dedication was taken.

Martin used the fashionable Byzantine basilica as his inspiration, but produced an original design with a central dome in a squat tower, but with a much taller west tower. The design seemed to excite interest, although

the cost of building the whole would have been very expensive. It was therefore decided to omit the western tower and the first of the two bays which had been designed for the nave, and the lady chapel which was to have been to the north of the sanctuary. The church is constructed of red brick with concrete domes and vaults. The external impression of the reduced church is not striking, but internally there are vistas presented by the vaulting. The transepts were converted in the 1930s to become chapels: one of them was made into a lady chapel, so obviating the need for the original plan to be completed. In the 1970s a nave altar was introduced and in 1978 a new brick porch was added at the west end (where the tower should have gone): regrettably the extension jars with the rest of the church. As originally built, there was little colour within but the addition of various Anglo-Catholic furnishings over the years has brightened the interior. There is a large Christus Rex over the high altar and a powerful set of stations of the cross.

Reference: Richardson, p. 86.

CHURCHES NOT REQUIRING FULL ENTRIES

The Ascension, Pollards Hill, Mitcham
A hall/church was erected in Sherwood Park Road in 1936: this was relegated to use as a hall in 1951 when a permanent church was erected.

St James the Apostle, Merton
A brick hall/church designed by T.F. Ford was erected in 1934 in Beaford Grove. It has an octagonal bell-turret, and was better constructed than many such. In 1957 a permanent church was built adjoining it and the first building reverted to use as a hall.

NEWHAM

St Andrew, Beckton

Status: demolished.
Former location: Roman Road.
Constructed: 1934.
Architect: not known.

This was a mission church of St Michael, Beckton, which itself has now disappeared. It was built in 1934 on land donated by J. Stokes & Sons but had a short life. It was closed in 1952 and in 1957 was sold for £450, which does not suggest there was any great architectural importance to the building.

Reference: VCHE, 6, p. 29.

St Barnabas, West Silvertown

Status: demolished.
Former location: between Eastwood and Westwood Roads.
Constructed: 1926.
Architects: Dawson, Son & Allerdyce.

In 1882 a wooden mission church was built in this area. In 1917 it was wrecked by the massive Silvertown ammunition explosion, which killed many people in the area. In 1919 a temporary hall was erected but in 1926 this was incorporated into a new church designed by local architects and used as the nave. An institute was alongside. Surviving pictures show a neo-Gothic

building of no great distinction. In 1934 a bell from the demolished church at Marks Hall, near Coggeshall, was donated. The area became depopulated after the Second World War and the church was administered from an adjoining parish before being demolished in the 1960s after a short life. The entire surroundings have now been redeveloped. There is more information on this corner of London in G. Hill and H. Bloch: *Silvertown Explosion* (Tempus, 2003) and H. Bloch: *Newham Dockland* (Chalford Publishing, 1995).

Reference: VCHE, 6, p. 123.

St Cedd, Canning Town

Status: derelict but under restoration.
Location: Newham Way, north side, near junction with Denmark Street.
Nearest station: Canning Town.
Constructed: 1938.
Architect: Gordon O'Neill.

In 1903 a brick hall, paid for by Richard Foster who was generous in his support of church building particularly in Walthamstow, was erected in this area, and in 1936 a new parish was formed. The church was built in 1938 to the memory of the Rev. T. Varney, the first mission curate, and his sister. O'Neill designed a substantial Romanesque-style building of red brick with a square tower at the south-western corner with castellated turret and a large asymmetrical gable over the entrance and baptistery. The nave windows are tall and there were no

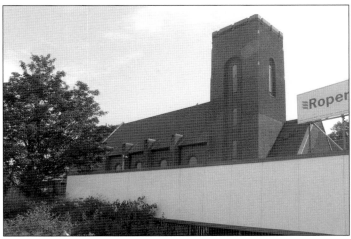

aisles, although two separate chapels. The brickwork is particularly fine around the doors and is thought to have been influenced by contemporary work in the Netherlands. The tradition was Anglo-Catholic.

The parish was split by the increasing traffic on the A13 immediately outside the church, and then in 1995 there was a serious fire affecting the organ. It was then decided that the cost of rebuilding both the church and the hall (which although built only in the 1970s was leaking) was excessive and since then vandals have wrecked more. It looked as though it was to be left to fall to pieces, but in the summer of 2005 the Ghana Seventh Day Adventist Church began renovation works in order to bring it back into use.

References: Pevsner, 5, p. 258; VCHE, 6, p. 123.

SS. George & Ethelbert, East Ham

Status: in use.
Location: Between Burford and Buxton Roads.
Nearest station: Upton Park.
Constructed: 1937.
Architects: Newberry & Fowler.

In 1914 a temporary hall was erected in Buxton Road and this became a parish church in 1923. The present very substantial church was erected largely as a result of an unusual project of cooperation between the Dioceses of Chelmsford and of Hereford: the latter

had little need for new churches at the time. Over half the cost was raised by that diocese and the Bishop of Hereford laid the foundation stone on 9 May 1936. Ethelbert was an Essex man martyred in Herefordshire, so he was added as dedicatee. The cruciform pattern of the church with squat central tower was even inspired by Hereford Cathedral. Newberry & Fowler provided their usual careful touches to the brickwork although the windows on this occasion were of Early English design. There is a lady chapel with its own roof. Apart from an additional entrance area which has been added to the west, the church is externally little altered. Inside too little has been altered since the church was built and internal subdivision has been avoided. There is a variety of stained glass of higher quality than often found. The tradition is central. This is an impressive and hidden church, in back streets where the casual traveller will not see it.

References: Pevsner, 5, p. 268; VCHE, 6, p. 30.

SS. George & Helena, Canning Town

Status: in use as Pentecostal church.
Location: Vincent Street, north side.
Nearest station: Canning Town.
Reconstructed: 1930.
Architect: Geoffrey Raymond.

The Malvern College Mission in Canning Town was founded in 1894 but was substantially extended and rebuilt after the First World War. The chapel was replaced by this very substantial new building in 1929-30: H.R.H. Princess Mary laid the foundation stone in April 1929. The new chapel was dedicated to SS. George

& Helena and was constructed to a very old-fashioned Gothic style by Raymond, although properly described in the latest *Buildings of England* as 'breathtaking' inside because of the hammer-beam roof which spans the whole width. There is a very large neo-Perpendicular (liturgically) west window and a massive rose window in the opposite wall, which faces on to Cooper Street. There are contemporary and later stained glass windows, some showing local workers. The mission later became the Mayflower Centre and has now been taken over by the New Rivers Christian Centre.

References: Pevsner, 5, p. 262; VCHE, 6, pp. 121, 141.

St Paul, East Ham

Status: in use.
Location: Burges Road, corner of Watson Avenue.
Nearest station: East Ham.
Constructed: 1932.
Architect: Charles Spooner.

The substantial growth in population in East Ham was between 1901 and 1911. In 1908 the development of the Burges Estate required a mission hall, which still stands. In 1911 a building fund was started and in 1924 a separate parish was formed, but it was not until the arrival of the dynamic Rev. R.P. Wernham in 1928 that real progress began to be made. He procured sponsorship for this project from the Girls' Friendly Society, who agreed to furnish the new building, which was designed by Charles Spooner and built in red brick at an angle to the hall. The original appeal to the GFS shows a church with a tall tower but, as in so many other cases, that was never built. Instead, there is a campanile at the west end of the south aisle, which itself had to be built shorter than the nave because of the confines of the site: the bells came from a demolished church at Wenden Lofts in north-west Essex.

The windows are round arched and in the absence of much external funding the detail was simple. Only one aisle was constructed, which is separated from the

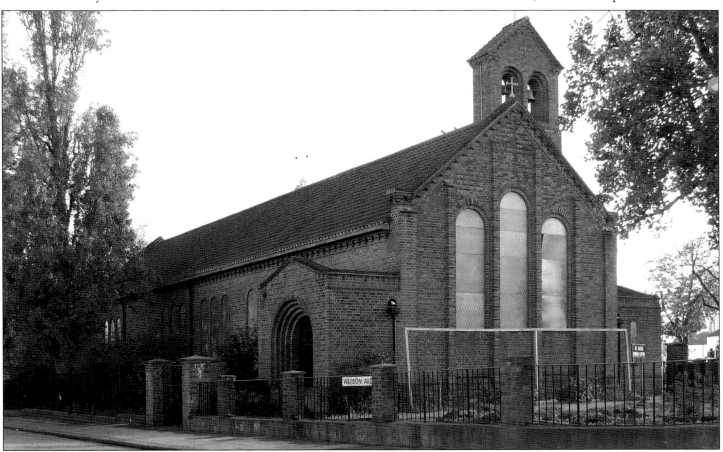

church itself by tapered concrete columns, and has its own side altar. The high altar was backed with a tall dossal which was lit by concealed windows either side of an arch. In 1987 a glass screen was inserted to form a separate lounge at the west end, and then in 1993 a foyer was erected to link the church and the hall: this has no doubt had beneficial consequences for the community, but has detracted from the perspective of the church itself. In 2002 redecoration took place internally with the result that the walls are now a sickly pale yellow.

References: Pevsner, 5, p. 271; VCHE, 6, p. 29; NCI, p. 45.

St Stephen, Stratford

Status: bombed and rebuilt as Hindu Temple.
Location: Cedars Road, north side.
Constructed: 1916.
Architect: not known.

This was a mission church of the Evangelical St John, Stratford. An iron church was replaced by a brick building: the Chelmsford Diocesan Chronicle records that the foundation stone was laid on 8 July 1916 and it was dedicated early the next year. The area had too many churches and after being bombed in 1943 it was not rebuilt. It is now used by Hindus, although it is not clear how much remains of the original building.

Reference: VCHE, 6, p. 119.

REDBRIDGE

St Andrew, Great Ilford

Status: in use.
Location: The Drive, corner of St Andrew's Road.
Nearest station: Redbridge.
Constructed: 1923.
Architect: Sir Herbert Baker.

A hall was provided for this pleasant area with middle class housing in 1906. In 1924 the hall was replaced by this impressive church designed as a memorial to Bishop Edgar Jacob of St Albans, in which diocese Ilford had been until the creation of the see of Chelmsford. Nothing was stinted in this building, unusually for the period, and particularly for the time of its construction, when money was generally in short supply. The builder, A.P. Griggs, later Mayor of Ilford, carried the work out

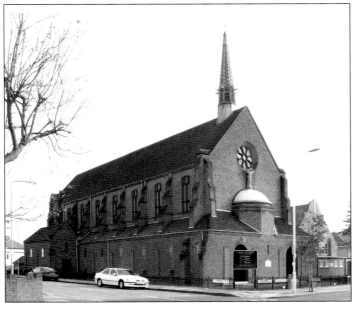

at cost and the north chapel is a memorial to his family: he himself was given a tablet after his death in 1957.

Sir Herbert Baker, distinguished for his monumental and governmental work around the Empire, designed a very tall nave with a flèche at the west end: the red-brick church thus proclaims itself above the suburban houses around. The sanctuary is within a large high apse and there is a small baptistery apse at the west end, above which but externally stands a figure of Peace by Sir Charles Wheeler. There are narrow aisles and clerestory windows above. The furnishings are of an equally high standard with stained glass by Karl Parsons, including a particularly fine window of Our Lady with the traditional lily, and by William Aikman. This is a building of high quality which has been well maintained and has not been subjected to insensitive modifications.

References: Pevsner, 5, p. 336; VCHE, 5, p. 257.

St Cedd, Barkingside

Status: in use.
Location: Marston Road, corner of Chalgrove Crescent.
Nearest station: South Woodford.
Constructed: 1938.
Architect: not known.

This is a typical red-brick hall/church in a typical area of bungalow development. It was intended that a permanent church be built on an adjoining site, but

this has never happened. The most prominent feature of the building is a white cross on a blue background on the west wall. The windows are simple and oblong. It no doubt has the advantage of being cheap to run and flexible in use, unlike many of its more illustrious neighbours.

Reference: VCHE, 5, p. 259.

St Francis of Assisi, Barkingside

Status: in use as hall.
Location: Fencepiece Road, east side, south of junction with Trelawney Road.

Nearest station: Hainault.
Constructed: 1935.
Architect: not known.

A marquee was replaced in 1935 by a hall set well back from the road, which received the fashionable contemporary dedication to St Francis. In 1956 J.J. Crowe built a red-brick permanent church in front of the hall, which itself looks as though it was a product of the interwar years and has nods towards the Spanish Mission style sometimes found at that time. The hall has decayed over the years and is about to be demolished in order to allow for the redevelopment of the land behind. It has a low roof and a brick cross over a roundel window on the west wall. The parish is strongly Anglo-Catholic in tone.

References: VCHE, 5, p. 259.

St George, Barkingside

Status: in use.
Location: Woodford Avenue, corner of Gantshill Crescent.
Nearest station: Gants Hill.
Constructed: 1932.
Architect: Sir Charles Nicholson.

Nicholson's church replaced an iron mission church of 1899 and a larger temporary church of 1927. Although it has a prominent position on the main road, it is not one of his more notable compositions. The church is of red brick with a squat tower at the west end topped by a two-stage copper roof with louvring between the stages. The building itself is long and low, with a number of neo-Jacobean windows on each side. The interior is

St Laurence, Barkingside

Status: in use.
Location: Hamilton Avenue, south side, corner of Donington Avenue.
Nearest station: Newbury Park.
Constructed: 1940.
Architect: N.F. Cachemaille-Day.

more successful than the exterior, with white walls and octagonal columns and panelled ceilings. The original high altar has fabric hangings although the inevitable nave altar has been placed in front of it. There is stained glass by William Aikman in the five-light east window.

References: Pevsner, 5, p. 328; VCHE, 5, p. 259.

This interesting church by Cachemaille-Day, more traditional than many of his designs, is hidden in a maze of semi-detached properties. It replaced an iron mission

church of 1890 which was in turn superceded by a hall of 1934 next to the permanent church. The church is arresting both internally and externally, although because of the war it was left unfinished and has never been completed. It is of light brown brick with a squat tower at the crossing, which it was intended should rise higher. It is however topped by a spire with narrow louvred lucarnes on each of its four faces. The windows and the arches within are of simple round-arched construction of no particular period, although the total effect is both pleasing and ecclesiastical. The east end was left as a stub which could be extended to a more dignified chancel if required, which results in a rather unsatisfactory brick screen behind the high altar.

References: Pevsner, 5, p. 329; VCHE, 5, p. 259.

St Luke, Great Ilford

Status: in use.
Location: Baxter Road, corner of Lowbrook Road.
Nearest station: Ilford.
Constructed: 1915.
Architect: E.T. Dunn.

A church hall, which remains in use, was erected in 1909 and was rapidly followed by a permanent church designed by local architect E.T. Dunn, which has been much altered over the years. The architect's original plan for a cruciform construction was never completed and the east wall was left as unfinished rough brick with a view to a chancel being added. Not only is that now impossible, because housing has been built right up to the wall, but in 1983 the orientation of the church was totally reversed and the altar is now beneath the four light west window and immediately in front of the three lancets, which, unusually, are beneath the main window. Meeting rooms and the like were inserted at the east end. Even before that the church did not reflect what was originally there, as it was almost completely wrecked by a bomb in 1940 and the parishioners had to return to the hall until reconstruction to the original design had taken place: this was not completed until 1954. Despite these mishaps, the quality of the original red brick neo-Gothic design has been preserved and the furnishings reflect a moderate Anglo-Catholicism against a background of whitewashed walls.

References: Pevsner, 5, p. 337; VCHE, 5, p. 257.

St Paul, Goodmayes

Status: in use.
Location: Barley Lane, west side, north of junction with Atholl Road.
Nearest station: Goodmayes.
Additions: 1917.
Architects: Chancellor & Son.

St Paul, Goodmayes, is a large neo-Perpendicular church in red brick on a main road. It qualifies for

this book because it was built in stages in 1903, 1917 and 1929 and such substantial work was done on the latter two occasions, although in accordance with the original design, that it is in large measure a church of

the period under discussion. The architects were based in Chelmsford. In 1903 the south chapel and aisle were built, then in 1917 the nave was added and it became a parish church. In 1929 the north aisle, baptistery and chancel were completed. There is a squat tower over the southern entrance, which was intended to be built higher but that has never been done. The design was old fashioned by the time it was finished, but the Gothic was competently executed. It has maintained an Anglo-Catholic tradition which sets it aside from most local parishes. There is a great deal of stained glass, some by Morris & Co.

References: Pevsner, 5, p. 331; VCHE, 5, p. 258.

RICHMOND

All Hallows, Twickenham

Status: in use.
Location: Chertsey Road, south side, between Whitton Road and London Road.
Nearest station: Twickenham.
Constructed: 1939.
Architect: R. Atkinson.

The driver speeding out of London on the A316 may well be surprised to see, on his left hand side, a tower by Christopher Wren which looks for all the world as if it had been moved bodily from the City. If he were to stop and enquire, he would find that indeed it has. This is the former tower of All Hallows, Lombard Street, a church which was almost hidden in later years by the offices which had been built all around it. It was made redundant shortly before the Second World War, and on sale the proceeds were used for the new suburbs.

It was to Twickenham that the tower itself migrated. The new church replaced a mission church: it was an extreme example of the attempts to establish continuity between ancient churches and the new areas. The architect was Robert Atkinson, who was also involved in a somewhat similar project with St Catherine Coleman, Hammersmith, but who was better known for his cinemas and other such buildings. The new nave and chancel are separate from the tower, but connected to it by a low passageway. The new building is a cleanly designed basilica with sharply-pitched roof and simple arched windows with round arches within. It forms an effective background for the many items brought from the City, including the pulpit, font with cover, candelabra, reredos (of 1880) altar table organ with case, charity board, royal arms, benches, sword rests and many monuments. There is also a candelabrum by Comper from St John, Red Lion Square, Bloomsbury. Atkinson also built the vicarage in similar style and forming part of the same group as the church and tower.

References: Pevsner, 2, p. 537; VCHM, 3, p. 161.

All Saints, East Sheen

Status: in use.
Location: East Sheen Avenue, east side, corner of Park Avenue.
Nearest station: Mortlake.
Constructed: 1929.
Architect: Newberry & Fowler.

This is another safe building from the hands of the Newberry partnerships. Kenneth Richardson explains how an earlier, more daring but probably very expensive, design by J.B.L. Tolhurst was rejected and Newberry & Fowler were chosen in his stead because of their recent success with St Mary, Sanderstead, and St Paul, Furzedown. The partnership, true to form, produced a

sound but not very inspired Gothic design which has lasted well. Again true to form, they designed a substantial tower which has never been built: the church does however have a small bell flèche. The nave and chancel have a continuous roof over them. The interior was of unremarkable but typical finish of grey brick and white stone. In 1965 there was a fire which necessitated considerable rebuilding and at the same time the altar was brought forward and the choir stalls placed behind it in the former sanctuary. More recently still however a rare reversal to the original plan has occurred, and the altar has been repositioned in its proper place and elevated.

References: Pevsner, 2, p. 470; Richardson, p. 43.

St Mark, Teddington

Status: in use.
Location: St Mark's Road, corner of Down Road.
Nearest station: Hampton Wick.
Reconstructed: 1938.
Architect: Cyril Farey.

References: Pevsner, 2, p. 535; VCHM, 3, p. 79; FMC, p. 48.

St Philip & All Saints, Kew

Status: in use.
Location: Atwood Avenue, corner Marksbury Avenue.
Nearest station: Kew Gardens.
Constructed: 1929.
Architect: Edward Swan.

This is an imposing building, regrettably hidden off the beaten track. It employs a similar construction to Farey's almost contemporary St Peter, Grange Park, with a squat central tower. The grey brick gives it a spacious feel, and the tower has round windows on the north and south sides: the nave has very plain square headed windows. The interior has echoes of the Romanesque. On the west wall is a large concrete statue of St Mark. Some benches were brought here from St John, Great Marlborough Street. The interior has a variety of Anglo-Catholic furnishings of a moderate type.

The reconstruction of an old barn to form St Philip & All Saints, Kew, was a logical conclusion of the Arts & Crafts Movement which had flowered before the First World War. The project was initiated by Uvedale Lambert and his wife Cecily with the intention of commemorating members of her family, the Hoares. They were much involved with church affairs and a later Uvedale Lambert was a guardian of the Shrine of Our Lady of Walsingham. The timber barn, previously standing on Lambert land at Stonehall Farm, Hurst Green, Oxted, Surrey, was taken down and reconstructed so that as far as possible the major beams were in similar positions to those in which they had stood since about the seventeenth century. The bricks and roof

interior, with its massive timbers in all directions, is quite unlike almost any other church and save for the contemporary St Alban, Cheam, the ideas behind this reconstruction remained unique. It is an extraordinary sight, particularly when considered with knowledge of the date it was erected.

References: Pevsner, 2, p. 471; NCI, p. 64; Richardson, p. 104.

tiles were baked specially in accordance with practice at the time the barn was constructed, and other timber was used, some from stables which had stood next to the barn. The tower was also based on an appropriate precedent. The external effect is curiously appropriate to the sylvan suburb where the church stands. The

CHURCH NOT REQUIRING A FULL ENTRY

Church Hall, Barnes
A hall/church without dedication was built by Clifton Davy in 1929 in simple Gothic style but with square topped windows on the sides. It was closed in 1940 and since the war has been adapted for secular use. A new porch has been added. See Richardson, p. 26.

SUTTON

All Saints, Hackbridge

Status: in use.
Location: London Road, between Orchard Avenue and
New Road.
Nearest station: Hackbridge.
Constructed: 1931.
Architect: H.P. Burke-Downing.

This church, sometimes known as All Saints, Beddington, was designed by Burke-Downing in his usual somewhat academic Gothic, although the church is less impressive than some because of the absence of a tower beyond a small bellcote at the west end, or indeed of any great height to the building. It replaced an iron church. The layout was entirely conventional, the exterior was of dark purple bricks and the interior is plastered. For all its utter conventionality, the church is pleasing and well kept. It stands in a small patch of green on the main road. The indefinable quality of looking as a church ought is found in this and indeed all his churches.

References: Pevsner, 2, p. 639; Richardson, p. 74.

Bishop Andrewes Church, St Helier

Status: in use.
Location: Wigmore Road, opposite Welhouse Road.
Nearest station: Carshalton.
Constructed: 1933.
Architect: Geddes Hyslop.

This is an interesting building, regrettably well concealed from anyone but the most persistent church crawler, and also now little used for worship: the Anglican services are once a fortnight, although weekly a Pentecostalist group meet. The building is cruciform, with long arms west and east, the latter containing the sanctuary, and shallow transepts. The tower is low and

squat and makes extensive use of reinforced concrete, as happens with the arches below. The architect also used ornamental brickwork on the exterior. There were other ingenious touches, such as a lantern in the tower and beneath it, on the floor of the crossing, a cross set in oak and ebony. Bishop Andrewes himself and his contemporaries, Laud, Hooker and Herbert, were commemorated in the reredos. The decline in the congregation, particularly marked here, has led in more recent years to the church hall being disposed of, the western section of the church being used as a hall, and most worship taking place only in the eastern arm, with the area under the crossing being used if required. Thus

all of the architect's spatial awareness has been severely compromised.

References: Pevsner, 2, p. 654; Richardson, p. 128.

Good Shepherd, Carshalton Beeches

Status: in use.
Location: Queen Mary's Avenue, corner Gaynesford Road.
Nearest station: Carshalton Beeches.
Constructed: 1930.
Architect: Martin Travers & T. F. W. Grant.

On 26 June 1929 Lord Halifax, the veteran leader of the Anglo-Catholic Movement, laid the foundation stone of one of the most unusual churches built between the wars. The Good Shepherd replaced a tin mission church of which Father Hope Patten of Walsingham had been in charge in 1920-1. It was a daughter church to All Saints, which is in the old village of Carshalton where the rector was the leading Papalist, W. Robert

Corbould, whose incumbency stretched from 1919 to 1958.

It was built in a loose expression of the Spanish Mission style, a form rarely found in this country. John Betjeman referred to the church as 'Essoldo moderne in a Hispano-Italian baroque style with clever stained glass. Displeasingly decayed but the essential quality of the design should not be ignored.' (The decay has been remedied since that was written.) The church is of brick, limewashed inside with rectangular metal Crittall-type windows. The roof is supported on steel principals and is covered with copper, with a large Spanish style bellcote on the west gable. The church was built astonishingly cheaply: the total cost of the structure was only £6,060, and of the fittings £700, and these were below the original estimates. The real error of the builders, however, was in not providing a damp course, and the buttresses, which are a distinctive feature of the external design, are hollow and useless, so the church suffered from damp from the time it was built. In due course the water penetration required a major restoration, which was carried out in 1984-5.

The ceiling is moulded pre-cast plaster and was originally stencilled in a baroque design, which has now unfortunately been painted over following the new work. Under the high circular east window hangs an enormous Italian-style rood above a simple wooden reredos resembling a type of pleated leatherwork, with an IHS monogram as the central design surrounded by a sunburst. The reredos and altar originally stood within somewhat incongruous riddel posts and on the altar were six baroque candlesticks and a crucifix. In 1952 part of the roof blew off in high winds. In 1967 the church suffered a fire in the vestries following vandalism, after which the riddels with their cherubs were removed and the altar pulled forward in order to allow celebration from the westward position. Travers himself gave the window of St Nicholas to the parish and opposite, in the south wall, is another window by him showing Our Lady crowned Queen of Heaven standing with a crescent moon under her feet. In the south-west porch is a rebus for Father Corbould showing a rook (Cor-) and the cricket bails flying (bowled). The other porch window has the arms of the Bishop of Southwark; following some internal reconstruction this window is now in a lavatory. The church is now independent of All Saints and the churchmanship has changed. However the building is now in a very good state, and in 2001 an extension was built to provide a chapel which was in the original plans but was never built.

References: Pevsner, 2, p. 646; NCI, p. 94; Richardson, p. 21.

St Alban, Cheam

Status: in use.
Location: Gander Green Lane, corner of Elmbrook Road, south side.
Nearest station: West Sutton.
Reconstructed: 1930.
Architects: Edward Swan and C.J. Marshall.

This church is a rebuilding of a late mediaeval barn, in just the same way as had happened at Kew, and directed by the same architect, Edward Swan, who was joined

here by a local designer, Charles Marshall. The idea for the construction came to Marshall after he had seen St Philip & All Saints at Kew. A barn was acquired from Cheam Court Farm, which had been a farm attached to Henry VIII's Nonsuch Palace and reconstructed on site: the contractors eschewed the use of scaffolding in an imitation of mediaeval practice which would have delighted the most committed supporters of the Arts and Crafts Movement, as would the black-and-white work on the organ chamber, which protrudes towards the north-east corner. The internal effect is similar to that at Kew, but the woodwork is less impressive and

Use of the church is now shared with Methodists. The interior is spacious and somewhat old-fashioned for its date.

perhaps less obtrusive. The chancel and four bays of the nave were built initially, and then in 1933 the west end was completed with a substantial timbered porch and a small bell-tower. A strong Anglo-Catholic tradition is maintained.

References: Pevsner, 2, p. 651; Richardson, p. 28.

Reference: Pevsner, 2, p. 655.

St John the Baptist, Belmont

Status: in use.
Location: Avenue Road, corner Northdown Road.
Nearest station: Belmont.
Constructed: 1915.
Architects: Greenaway & Newberry.

This is a substantial Gothic church on the very southern outskirts of the built-up area, with no tower. The architects used pale brick and their usual neo-Decorated tracery in the large windows. An unusual feature for a church of this age is a clock above one of the windows.

St Patrick, Wallington

Status: in use.
Location: Park Hill Road, corner Glen End Road.
Nearest station: Wallington.
Reconstructed: 1932.
Architects: Newberry & Fowler.

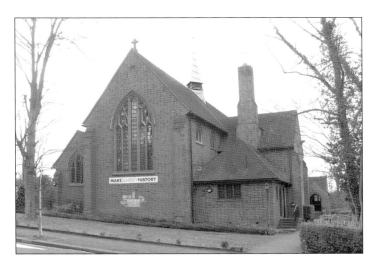

This prosperous-looking area of Wallington has a standard Newberry & Fowler brick Gothic church, very similar to those at Furzedown and Sanderstead and even more similar to the then recently built All Saints, East Sheen. It has a chancel with aisles and a small bell tower. The interior here was largely brick, with little use either of stone or plaster, just as at Sheen. The church has never been consecrated, because Bishop Garbett wanted to secure the patronage for the Diocese, and

was unwilling to consecrate it until that had been settled. Wallington was however an Evangelical parish and the holders of the living, the Church Society Trust, did not wish to relinquish it. The interior is correspondingly devoid of adornment.

Reference: Richardson, p. 171.

St Peter, St Helier

Status: in use.
Location: Bishopsford Road, south side, between Middleton Road and Roche Walk.
Nearest station: St Helier.
Constructed: 1932.
Architect: Sir Charles Nicholson.

This is a very large church, although not as large as provided by Nicholson's original plans. It was built as the central church for the huge St Helier estate and given a prime position on the sprawling development and in

advance of houses being built around it. The church is lofty, with aisles on both sides but clerestory windows above them. Nicholson built here in the basilica style with relatively narrow neo-Romanesque windows. The west front has a large circular window and a bell-tower rising from it on the south side with copper roof. Inside the brick was whitewashed and there was extensive use of good oak, including to the front of the gallery at the west end and the roof, both of which were tastefully painted. The architect's brother, A.K. Nicholson, provided two windows in the lady chapel and Martin Travers designed windows and furnishings for a chapel of St Francis, but these unfortunately were never executed. Equally unfortunately, in 1973 the incumbent commissioned Peter Pelz, a self-taught artist, to paint Stations of the Cross in mural form, followed in 1977 by a huge mural depicting the Last Judgment, which disfigured the west front. Litigation followed, and in 1991 the Chancellor ordered the removal of the Stations but the retention of the external mural. The mural has now faded, which makes it, if anything, a worse eyesore. It entirely destroys the dignified façade which Nicholson intended, but the quality of the design can be seen from the interior.

References: Pevsner, 2, p. 654; NCI, p. 112; Richardson, p. 133.

CHURCHES NOT REQUIRING FULL ENTRIES

Church Hall, St Helier
A hall/church without dedication was built by Geddes Hyslop in 1930. It was larger than many such, and used some features which the same architect later used in Bishop Andrew's church. The hall was sold for use as a Youth Centre in 1963 but still stands: see Richardson, p. 125.

St Andrew, Carshalton
The exact date when the Rev. W.R. Corbould, rector of Carshalton for many years and a strong upholder of Papalism within the Church of England, had the mission church of St Andrew in Wrythe Lane built is not clear, but it was a small temporary building which suitably furnished for the propagation of the religion of the parish. It achieved notoriety after Father Corbould's death when Bishop Stockwood effectively ejected the elderly curate, Father Rice Harris, and closed the church, which was then demolished.

St Oswald, Cheam
In 1936 a hall/church was built by T.P. Carr for this area, which was developed on the site of the Brock's fireworks factory. A church was added in 1953 but the hall remains standing.

WALTHAM FOREST

Emmanuel, Leyton

Status: in use.
Location: Lea Bridge Road, corner of Hitcham Road.
Nearest station: St James Street Walthamstow.
Constructed: 1936.
Architects: Martin Travers & T.F.W. Grant.

The third new church built by Travers & Grant was Emmanuel. A model of this church was exhibited at the Royal Academy in 1934. It was constructed very cheaply, the total cost being only £5,102, with £474 for fittings: part was defrayed by local masonic lodges. Regrettably the frugal specification has meant constant problems with damp penetration. The church is of brick construction with pre-cast tracery. The window lights have rounded tops, and the tracery of pale stone stands out against the brick. Around the door frames there is stylised decoration in the stone, with a faint baroque flavour. The roof was wooden with copper over; however, the copper has since been removed. A cupola was planned, but was never added and the aisle roofs are of pre-cast concrete slabs with an asphalt outer covering.

Travers installed a large gilded reredos with a plain centre panel and on the side panels were characteristic tassel decorations. On the altar stood a plain cross, but no candlesticks, as these were not required for this Evangelical stronghold. The reredos has since been repainted, apparently on the suggestion of the wife of a previous vicar, in a lurid orange and green, with a large wooden cross in front of it, but the remainder of the church is relatively untouched. There is a considerable quantity of good woodwork in the pews, choir stalls, and pulpit, and there are two windows by Travers, one of St George and the Dragon and one of coats of arms with a dedication to the chairman of the building committee for the church. The church was specifically designed with no windows on the main road side, in order to cut down on noise. The church has a high circular window above the altar and an organ in the west

gallery. The adjoining vicarage is also by Travers and again is of cheaply built construction with a flat roof.

References: Pevsner, 5, p. 727; VCHE, 6, p. 222; NCI, p. 42.

St Augustine of Hippo, Leytonstone

Status: demolished.
Former location: Lincoln Street.
Reconstructed: 1920.
Architect: not known.

This low-built, unobtrusive church was built in 1902, but had a considerable curiosity value, in that it was the only church in London destroyed by bombing in the First World War. A firebomb from a Zeppelin caused it to be almost entirely burnt out, and there was no insurance which covered the damage. Extensive renovation was required while the hall was used. The church had an Anglo-Catholic tradition. It was demolished when in the 1980s the parish was united to that of Holy Trinity, Harrow Green.

Reference: VCHE, 6, p. 220.

St Edmund King & Martyr, South Chingford

Status: in use.
Location: Larkswood Road, north side, near junction with Chingford Mount Road.
Nearest station: Highams Park.
Constructed: 1939.
Architect: N.F. Cachemaille-Day.

St Edmund is a more traditional work than some of its architect's other productions, but still interesting. It has a crossing tower over the chancel which lights the area beneath. There are finely detailed Perpendicular windows and they together with the brick and flint construction give more than a look of East Anglia to the church. Inside there are original fittings by the architect, although there was some reordering in the early 1950s which involved resiting the font and a war memorial. There is an east window by Christopher Webb, and the lady chapel and the south transept have

windows by Lawrence Lee. Cachemaille-Day himself designed the window of Christ the Light of the World. There are three surviving panels by Clayton & Bell from the former Merchant Seaman's Orphanage at Wanstead: others were installed when the church was built but were blown out in the war. This is a regrettably little-known church, just off a main road.

References: Pevsner, 5, p. 713; VCHE, 5, p. 111.

St John, Walthamstow

Status: in use.
Location: Brookscroft Road, corner of Chingford Road.
Nearest station: Walthamstow Central.
Constructed: 1924.
Architect: H.P. Burke-Downing.

This church illustrates a great deal of what has occurred in the Church of England over the last eighty years. Immediately after the First World War there was an

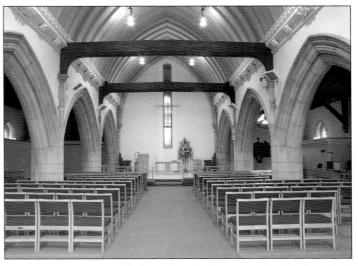

impassioned appeal by the Diocese of Chelmsford to replace the church of 1830, which was in serious danger of collapse. The population of the area had increased greatly and a large new building was required. H.P. Burke-Downing was commissioned to design the replacement, which cost the then astronomical sum of £23,000, more than double the cost of the average church in this book. Burke-Downing produced a large church in his scholarly neo-Gothic, using Crowborough brick with dressings of Portland stone and a single roof over nave and chancel with a separate lady chapel. Even with the amount spent, the church was not completed: only three bays of the projected four were built and galvanised iron sheets formed the west wall. In 1936 a cottage in front of the church was demolished and the frontage opened out, but it was not until 1960 that sufficient money was raised to complete the design with a fourth bay and a permanent west wall, the work of John Phillips. The new wall has a fine rose window over five lancets. The high hopes of that era soon fell away and in 1996 a substantial reordering took place which has resulted in a new floor being inserted to divide the church horizontally: the upper area is used for worship. The chancel was also divided at the same time. Thus within a generation the same church was substantially extended and then even more substantially reduced in size. There is more information on this and other local churches in W.G.S. Tonkin: *The Anglican Church in* *Walthamstow* (Walthamstow Antiquarian Society, 1963).

References: Pevsner, 5, p. 745; VCHE, 6, p. 292.

WANDSWORTH

St Augustine, Tooting

Status: in use.
Location: Broadwater Road, north side, north of Upper Tooting Road.
Nearest station: Tooting Broadway.
Constructed: 1929.
Architect: H.P. Burke-Downing.

This church was built to replace two halls which had successively catered for the area, which had expanded with the construction of the Totterdown estate before the First World War. The foundation stone was laid by the Duchess of York on 30 November 1929. The designs of the architect, H.P. Burke-Downing, were in his customary scholarly Gothic and had been scaled down slightly since the project was first proposed. He, as usual, adequately reproduced the fourteenth century in twentieth-century brick and stone. The church has a nave, aisles on each side, and a chancel with vestry on

one side and a chapel on the other: an utterly conventional layout. There is no tower, but a small campanile. The windows are of simple Decorated type, the walls plastered. It was damaged in the war and rebuilt to the same design.

References: Pevsner, 2, p. 697; NCI, p. 98; Richardson, p. 167.

St John The Divine, Earlsfield

Status: in use.
Location: Garratt Lane, west side, north of junction with St John's Drive.
Nearest station: Earlsfield.
Constructed: 1915.
Architects: Greenaway & Newberry.

This unprepossessing building was built as a temporary church, but has never been replaced. It in turn replaced an iron mission church. It is low in construction although not in the religion practised inside, and has a nave and chancel under one roof, and a simple but effective five-light window in the west wall. The north porch has been modified in recent years (c.1984) with a rather ugly gable, and there is a hall attached on the south side built about 1962 with the insurance money from the destruction by fire of the original iron mission. The west wall of the church is right on the main road, but here Greenaway & Newberry's Gothic is at its least demonstrative. It does however have the advantage

of being easy and cheap to heat and clean, advantages denied more glamorous buildings.

References: none.

St Margaret, Putney

Status: in use.
Location: Putney Park Lane, corner of Church Walk.
Nearest station: Barnes.
Reconstructed: 1926.
Architect: W.A. Forsyth.

This church has a very unusual history. It was built in 1873 as a private Nonconformist chapel, being used first by Baptists and then by Presbyterians, but after a period of disuse was acquired by the Church of England in 1910 as a chapel of ease. It was then a small Gothic building, orientated north/south with a small bell-tower. Renovation and the construction of a narthex took place, but its size was inadequate for the area: this inadequacy became more pressing when the Roehampton estate was planned, which was to be built very near the site. The substantial enlargement

Constructed: 1926.
Architects: Greenaway & Newberry.

of a chapel such as this proved to be a difficult design exercise. Burke-Downing was first approached, but his addition was thought to be too expensive. Eventually, after much wrangling, he was sacked and the choice fell on W.A. Forsyth. His scheme was actually very little cheaper, but he seems to have got on better with his clients, and the work proceeded. The effect was to add a new east end which doubled the size of the church. The nave was extended and a chancel with lady chapel and vestries was added. Although internally the conversion was very successful, externally the transition from old to new is very obvious, although a matching Gothic style was employed.

References: Pevsner, 2, p. 687; Richardson, p. 112.

St Paul, Furzedown

Status: in use.
Location: Welham Road, west of junction with Chillerton Road.
Nearest station: Tooting.

The Furzedown area, between Tooting and Streatham, was first developed before the First World War, and a hall by Greenaway & Newberry was erected in 1911. The same architects were invited to produce a permanent church and this was built in 1925-6. It is another standard production from the firm: careful, unadventurous red-brick Gothic, with no tower. There are lancet windows: those in the east end have fine glass by

Martin Travers to a Christ in Glory design almost identical to that which he installed at St Andrew, Langley Mill, Derbyshire. The church was damaged in the war and the window was blown out, but later restored. The interior has whitewashed stone arcades, which contrast with the brick. This is an unobtrusive but well-built construction.

Reference: Richardson, p. 72.

ARCHITECTS AND THEIR LONDON CHURCHES
1915–1945
Churches are listed with their district and London Borough.

ASHEAD & RAMSEY
1932: St Anselm, Kennington, Lambeth
ALDER, J.S.
1915: St Barnabas, Temple Fortune, Barnet
1916: St Catherine, Neasden, Brent
ANDREWS, P.M.
1936: St Martin, Barnehurst, Bexley
ASHFORD, T.N.
1932: St George, Morden, Morden
ATKINSON, R.
1922: St Catherine Coleman, Hammersmith, Hammersmith & Fulham
1939: All Hallows, Twickenham, Richmond
BAKER, SIR H.
1923: St Andrew, Ilford, Redbridge
BLOMFIELD & DRIVER
1915: St Thomas, Acton Vale, Ealing (A.C. Blomfield)
1926: St Thomas, Becontree, Barking & Dagenham
BURKE-DOWNING, H.P.
1924: St John, Walthamstow, Waltham Forest
1929: St Augustine, Tooting, Wandsworth
1931: All Saints, Hackbridge, Sutton
CACHEMAILLE-DAY, N.F.
1932: St Saviour, Eltham, Greenwich (Welch, Cachemaille-Day & Lander)
1935: St Mary, Becontree, Barking & Dagenham (Welch, Cachemaille-Day & Lander)
1936: St Paul, Ruislip, Hillingdon
1936: St Edward, Perivale Park, Ealing
1937: St Paul, South Harrow, Harrow
1938: St Anselm, Belmont, Harrow

1939: St Paul, Oxgate, Brent
1939: St Edmund, Chingford, Waltham Forest
1940: St Laurence, Barkingside, Redbridge
CARÖE & PASSMORE
1922: St Michael & All Angels, Mill Hill, Barnet
1927: St John the Divine, Romford, Havering
1934: St Oswald, Norbury, Croydon
1939: St Matthew, Muswell Hill, Haringey
CARR, T.P.
1937: St Oswald (hall), Cheam, Sutton
CHANCELLOR & SON
1917: St Paul (extension), Goodmayes, Redbridge
CHRISTMAS, E.C.
1925: Holy Trinity (hall), Sydenham, Lewisham
CORLETTE, H.C.
1926: St Anselm, Hayes, Hillingdon.
CROWE, J.J.
1933: All Saints (rebuilding), Squirrels Heath, Havering
1938: St Michael & All Angels, Gidea Park, Havering
1939: St Peter, Harold Wood, Havering
DAVY, C.R.
1929: Church Hall, Barnes, Richmond
DAWSON SON & ALLERDYCE
1926: St Barnabas, West Silvertown, Newham
DUNN, E.T.
1915: St Luke, Ilford, Redbridge
FAREY, C.A.
1932: St Michael, Tokyngton, Brent
1938: St Mark, Teddington, Richmond
1940: St Peter, Grange Park, Enfield
1941: All Hallows, North Greenford, Ealing

FORD, T.F.
1931: All Saints (extension), New Eltham, Greenwich
1933: St Barnabas (removal), Eltham, Greenwich
1933: St Michael, East Wickham, Bexley
1934: St George, Tolworth, Kingston
1934: St Mary, Welling, Bexley
1934: St James (hall), Merton, Morden
1935: St David (rebuilding), Lower Holloway, Islington
1935: St Michael (hall), Harrow Weald, Harrow
FORSYTH, W.A.
1926: St Margaret (extension), Putney, Wandsworth
1934: St Andrew (removal), Kingsbury, Brent
GEORGE TRUE & DUNN
1940: Christ Church, Orpington, Bromley
GIBBONS, J.H.
1933: St Francis of Assisi, Gladstone Park, Brent
1933: St Jerome, Dawley, Hillingdon
1936: St Mary, Kenton, Harrow
1939: St Barnabas, Northolt Park, Ealing
GREEN, W. CURTIS
1932: St George, Waddon, Croydon
GREENAWAY & NEWBERRY (NEWBERRY & FOWLER FROM 1927)
1915: St John the Baptist, Belmont, Sutton
1915: St James, Riddlesdown, Croydon
1915: St John the Divine, Earlsfield, Wandsworth
1926: St Mary, Sanderstead, Croydon
1926: St Paul, Furzedown, Wandsworth
1929: All Saints, East Sheen, Richmond
1932: St Martin, Dagenham, Barking & Dagenham
1932: St Patrick, Wallington, Sutton
1934: Good Shepherd, Collier Row, Havering
1934: St James, New Malden, Kingston
1935: St John the Divine, Selsdon, Croydon
1935: St Francis of Assisi, West Wickham, Bromley
1937: St Mary, Chelsfield, Bromley
1937: SS. George & Ethelbert, East Ham, Newham
1939: St John the Divine, New Malden, Kingston

HALL-JONES, F.
1923: St John (rebuilding), Ealing, Ealing
HARE, C.G.
1928: St Benet & All Saints (rebuilding), Kentish Town, Camden
1931: St Mildred, Addiscombe, Croydon
HELLICAR, E.A.
1926: St John the Evangelist, Welling, Bexley
HYSLOP, G.
1930: Church Hall, St Helier, Sutton
1933: Bishop Andrewes, St Helier, Sutton
JUPP, S.
1929: St Swithun (hall), Purley, Croydon
KENYON, A.W.
1936: St Alban, North Harrow, Harrow
LEY, A.S.R.
1932: Holy Redeemer, Lamorbey, Bexley
LYON, T.H.
1926: St Augustine, Wembley Park, Brent
MARTIN, A.C.
1931: St Olave, Mitcham, Morden
MARTIN-SMITH, D.F.
1936: John Keble, Mill Hill, Barnet
MATHEWS & RIDLEY
1926: St Francis of Assisi, Coulsdon, Croydon
MAUFE, SIR E.B.
1924: St Bede, Clapham, Lambeth
1924: St Saviour, Acton, Ealing
1934: St Thomas, Hanwell, Ealing
MEREDITH, E.
1931: St Christopher, Becontree, Barking & Dagenham
1931: St Peter, Becontree, Barking & Dagenham
MILNER & CRAZE
1934: St Alban, Becontree, Barking & Dagenham
1935: St George, Dagenham, Barking & Dagenham
1939: St Thomas, Oakwood, Enfield

MITCHELL & BRIDGWATER
1937: Ascension (hall), Preston, Brent
MULLINS, G.T.
1934: St Francis of Assisi, Petts Wood, Bromley
NICHOLAS & DIXON-SPAIN
1927: St Alphage, Burnt Oak, Barnet
NICHOLSON, SIR C.A.
1925: St Dunstan, Bellingham, Lewisham
1928: St John the Baptist, Southend, Lewisham
1928: St Barnabas, Downham, Lewisham
1929: St Andrew, Bromley, Bromley
1932: All Saints, Hillingdon, Hillingdon
1932: St Elisabeth, Becontree, Barking & Dagenham
1932: St Lawrence, Eastcote, Hillingdon
1932: St George, Barkingside, Redbridge
1932: St Peter, St Helier, Sutton
1937: St Luke, Downham, Lewisham
O'NEILL, G.G.
1938: St Cedd, Canning Town, Newham
PITE, A.B.
1915: St Saviour (hall), Ruskin Park, Lambeth
PITE, W., SON & FAIRWEATHER
1915: St Peter, Acton Green, Ealing (W.A.Pite)
1926: St Jude, Thornton Heath, Croydon
1933: Holy Cross, Hornchurch, Havering
1936: St John, Eden Park, Bromley
POWELL, G.S.
1933: St Augustine, Beckenham, Bromley
1934: St James (extension), Elmers End, Bromley
RAYMOND, G.
1930: SS. George & Helena, Canning Town, Newham
RICHARDSON, SIR A.E.
1939: Holy Cross, Greenford, Ealing
SCOTT, SIR G.G.
1933: St Alban, Golders Green, Barnet

SEELY & PAGET
1938: Ascension, Hanger Hill, Ealing
1938: All Saints, Heston, Hounslow
1939: St John the Baptist, Tottenham, Haringey
SHEARMAN, E.C.
1916: St Barnabas, North Ealing, Ealing
1929: St Gabriel, Acton, Ealing
1932: St Barnabas, Temple Fortune, Barnet
1933: St Francis of Assisi, Isleworth, Hounslow
SPOONER, C.
1932: St Paul, East Ham, Newham
SWAN, E.A.
1929: St Philip & All Saints, Kew, Richmond
1930: St Alban, Cheam, Sutton
TRAVERS, H.M.O.
1930: Good Shepherd, Carshalton Beeches, Sutton
1932: Holy Redeemer, Streatham Vale, Lambeth
1934: St Mary (hall), West Wickham, Bromley
1936: Emmanuel, Leyton, Waltham Forest
1938: St John the Baptist (extension), Greenhill, Harrow
WAYMOUTH, W.C.
1925: St Andrew, Sudbury, Brent
WELCH & LANDER
1938: St Martin, East Barnet, Barnet
WISEMAN, A.E.
1936: St John the Divine, Becontree, Barking & Dagenham
1940: St Patrick, Barking, Barking & Dagenham
WOOD, W.H.
1916: St Augustine, Belvedere, Bexley
WORTHINGTON, THOMAS, & SONS
1937: St Edward (hall), Mottingham, Bromley

AUTHORS

Michael Yelton was in practice as a barrister for 25 years and is now a Circuit Judge. He is the author of a number of books on ecclesiastical history and architecture, including *Martin Travers (1886-1948): an Appreciation* (jointly with Rodney Warrener) (Unicorn Press, 2003); *Anglican Papalism 1900-1960* (Canterbury Press, 2005); and *Alfred Hope Patten and the Shrine of Our Lady of Walsingham* (Canterbury Press, 2006). He is married with three adult children and lives in Cambridge.

John Salmon was a General Medical Practitioner in Enfield for 32 years until his retirement in 2000. Since then he has pursued his interest in church photography with a particular interest in stained glass. His work has appeared in a number of books and magazines dealing with ecclesiology, and also in various church guide books. He has been instrumental in setting up several church websites, where his photography has played a major part. He has carried out research on the life and works of the architect Ernest Charles Shearman, which at present remains unpublished.

INDEX

The main entries for churches may be easily found in the gazetteer under the appropriate London Borough and are therefore not indexed here. Architects are only indexed here in the case of references that could not be found by using the list on pp. 157-9.

162